AWESOME GRAMMAR

By

Becky Burckmyer

CAREER PRESS

Franklin Lakes, NJ

Interior illustrations by Sage Stossel, 2008.

AWESOME GRAMMAR
EDITED BY JODI BRANDON
TYPESET BY EILEEN DOW MUNSON
Cover design by The DesignWorks Group
Printed in the U.S.A. by Book-mart Press
EAN: 978-1-60163-043-8

To order this title, please call toll-free 1-800-CAREER-1 (NJ and Canada: 201-848-0310) to order using VISA or MasterCard, or for further information on books from Career Press.

The Career Press, Inc., 3 Tice Road, PO Box 687,
Franklin Lakes, NJ 07417
www.careerpress.com

Library of Congress Cataloging-in-Publication Data
Burckmyer, Becky.
    Awesome grammar / by Becky Burckmyer.
        p. cm.
    Includes index.
        1. English language—Grammar. 2. English language—Rhetoric.
    I. Title.

PE1112.B747 2008
428.2--dc22

                                                        2008034130

Contents

Part III: Appearance: Looking Good Is the Best Revenge

Introduction: What Is Grammar Anyway? And Who Cares?

First question: What is grammar? I'm glad you asked! Here's what grammar isn't, selected with special care from a full-page ad in the *Boston Globe* a few years back:

> Ask your banker why they can't guarantee your
> money in 13 days like [Nameless Bank] can!

If that looks pretty good to you, keep reading. That kind of writing can pigeonhole you as a **Writer Out of Control**. With as much writing as most of us are doing today, you can't afford to be viewed that way. The Internet Revolution means we now communicate more and more through the written word, rather than picking up the phone, walking down the hall, or setting up a meeting.

Grammar is the set of rules we use in spoken and written English. Because it's crucial to use the *same* set if we're going to communicate, we need to agree on what they are. Luckily for us, in the 18th century, when people were gripped by a mania for classifying and writing everything down, English grammar attained more or less its present form. It's kind of comforting to reflect that these rules change very slowly, when they change at all. But that means it's all the more essential to observe them carefully—not just for comfort, but also for the ability to communicate. For example, you won't communicate well if you write "Betsy was fearless: He liked to climb the rickety old water tower at night." Everyone will be wondering who *he* is. The rule behind this is that *he* is a pronoun that stands in for a male subject (as opposed, say, to someone named Betsy). Grammar is the set of agreed-upon rules that helps us make sense to one another in speech and in print.

Second question: Who cares? Well, I'm guessing you, for one, or you wouldn't be reading this. In fact a lot of people care. Don't for a minute believe that the Internet has revolutionized writing to the point where anything goes! If anything, grammar and correct writing are more important than ever because, as I said, we're writing more now than ever before. We can't afford to lose a reader's confidence by making errors, or worse, to be misunderstood.

If you observe the rules of grammar, your writing will be correct. It may not be as stylish as E.B. White, as poetic as William Shakespeare, or as captivating as John Grisham. If you're writing correctly and grammatically, though, two excellent things are likely to happen.

First, you'll be understood. It's much harder to misunderstand someone who is speaking or writing grammatically. The "Betsy/he" example comes to mind. Because it's ungrammatical, its meaning is ambiguous. Or take something such as this:

I write him that I were glad he caming.

You may think at first you understand what's being said, despite the ungrammatical verb tenses, but look closely. For example, is the letter to be or already written? Has he already come, or is he still to arrive? Are *him* and *he* one person or two? Several interpretations are possible, and most people don't want to interpret. They want to understand without having to think about it. So grammar promotes communication.

Second, you'll please the people who care about correct writing. These people are more numerous than you may think: The National Commission on Writing estimates that Corporate America spends $3.1 billion annually on remedial training for current and new employees (based on 2004 statistics). *Some*body sure cares—$3.1 billion worth. And often those who care are the people (your professor, your boss, your mortgage lender, your future father-in-law) who have decision-making power over you—which, frankly, is not a coincidence. People who write well tend to make it to the top. I should hang a big poster in my office: Good Grammar Will Make You CEO of Exxon Mobil Corp.

Observing the rules of grammar helps you get your message across to readers, and it charms—or at least fails to irritate—discriminating (non-pejorative synonym for picky) readers.

In my 20-some years as a consultant to businesses, I've met one—just one—CEO who was a really bad writer. That's not a lot. I've met a bunch, and most of them weren't just good writers, they liked to mud wrestle with grammar. Their eyes lit up when they talked about the damage inflicted on meaning by split infinitives, comma splices, and that sort of stuff. The CEO signed me on to help sharpen his employees' writing skills and to edit his own copy. The bottom line: People who write well—and even some who don't—place a high value on good writing by others.

I touch on the high points of grammar in this book, basically covering the rules. But wait—there's more. Some of the chapters cover writing issues that are not strictly in the realm of grammar, but that can nonetheless be dealt with correctly or resoundingly *in*correctly. These will mar your writing if you aren't aware of them, so, to make you correct beyond belief, I've included them. Such chapters as "The Right Word" (Chapter 10), for example, and "Parallel Construction" (Chapter 9), though they're not strictly about grammar, will help you avoid a "poor writer" label. If you heed the messages in this book, therefore, you're going to be scrupulously correct from just about any standpoint.

Good writing starts with grammar, the building blocks of the writing industry. So, shall we? I hope you enjoy *Awesome Grammar*, and I hope it's helpful.

PART I
PARTS OF SPEECH

Hold the Phone! Stuff You Need to Know

Humorist and grammarian Dave Barry once identified the parts of speech as the subject, the predator, the adjutant, the premonition, and the larynx. I think this is pretty funny, and I repeated it to one of my writing classes. To my horror, several people began writing it down.

All right, so you don't need to know the names of every part of speech, and, if you think the concept is deadly, I understand. In fact, I'm not planning to cover all of them. Far from it. Why should you wade into the definition of a gerund, and do you really need to be told how nouns work? However, the information about the six most familiar parts of speech that I've included in this section should be part of everyone's working knowledge. At least give each chapter a quick review: You might learn something, or discover you need to *un*learn something you learned back when.

Verbs:
Looking for Some Action

Verbs are of enormous importance because that's, you should pardon the expression, where the action is. They can infuse your writing with strength and excitement. You need to take advantage of these "hot spots" by using your verbs correctly. By the same token, if you squander or misuse your verbs, your writing will suffer.

First of all, your verb tenses must be correct. Verbs in English, as in most languages, change their endings depending on who's performing the action and whether the verb is something done in the past, present, or future. That's a vast oversimplification: English has a lot of tenses. Here are just a few important ones using the verb *to watch* as an example:

Present tense:	I watch	we watch
	you watch	you watch
	he, she, it watches	they watch
Simple past:	I watched	we watched
	you watched	you watched
	he, she, it watched	they watched
Present perfect:	I have watched	we have watched
	you have watched	you have watched
	he, she, it has watched	they have watched
Participle/gerund:	watching	

Make Sure You Know the Correct Forms for Verb Tenses

If only all our verbs conjugated the way *watch* does! Alas, English is notorious for the irregularity of its verbs. If there's even a chance that you don't always use the right verb form, check your dictionary. Check it often. There is no excuse, in speaking or writing, for such substandard English as the following:

> Mrs. Saunders says *she done* the work you wanted.
>
> *He come* over yesterday to see my new gyrating spectroscope.
>
> My nest egg *has shrank* with the stock market contractions.

When Describing an Event or Experience, Don't Switch Tenses

This can happen when the writer gets excited about what's going on:

> Getting ready to scale the wall, Eleanor *uncoiled* the climbing rope, nearly 200 feet long. She *put on* her harness, then knotted the rope onto it. At last she *begins* her ascent.

Of course it should be *began*. This error is especially common in photo captions, where a writer starts out in the present, then slips into the past tense (because the whole thing actually happened yesterday or last month):

> The president *shares* a light moment with the prime minister, who *was wearing* his country's traditional headgear and robe.

It should be *is wearing* (and let us hope the president wasn't laughing at the prime minister's outfit).

Be Sure Tenses Are in the Proper Order

If two things happened, but one happened at a significantly earlier time than the other, your verb tenses must show this distinction:

No: She *was* every inch a queen, and was raised to be so.

Yes: She *was* every inch a queen and *had been raised* to be so.

(The lady was raised before she became a queen.)

No: I *learned* that Meg's husband *died* far from home in Pakistan.

Yes: I *learned* that Meg's husband *had died* far from home in Pakistan.

> (His death happened first; the writer learned about it subsequently.)

Unvarying Truths: The Exception

However, if you're writing in the past tense and refer to something that has always been and always will be the case, you should use the present tense:

> Galileo *was* a follower of Copernicus, who *stated* that the earth *revolves* around the sun.
>
> I *reminded* Miranda that it *takes* two to make an argument.

Don't Use the Helping Verb *Did* if *Have* Works

No: *Did you get* your uniform in the mail already?

Yes: *Have you gotten* your uniform in the mail already?

No: *Did* Hector *ask* Amundson for a raise yet?

Yes: *Has* Hector *asked* Amundson for a raise yet?

Your clues are *yet* and *already*, which usually accompany this construction.

Learn to Use the Subjunctive Mood

The subjunctive verb form is increasingly rare today, but it shines up your writing nicely if you know how to use it. It can also be a weapon of minor destruction in ignorant hands: Using the subjunctive where it doesn't belong spoils the impression you're trying to give.

The chart on page 14 shows how the subjunctive looks. We'll take the verb *to be*, which is often used in the subjunctive mood.

It's the same with other verbs, though it shows only in *he*, *she*, and *it* (present): *he take, she find, it carry*, and the past imperfect, where *to be* is a helping verb: *I were carrying, she were riding*. You have my permission to think of that as another use of *to be* in the subjunctive and not to worry about the past imperfect.

	Present	Past
Singular	I be	I were
	you be	you were
	he, she, it be	he, she, it were
Plural	we be	we were
	you be	you were
	they be	they were

It looks strange: We don't say *we be* or *Donald take* in ordinary conversation. But this is now. The Elizabethans, Shakespeare, and his contemporaries high and low made frequent use of the subjunctive. Shakespeare wrote of his "dark lady":

> **The Subjunctive in Renaissance England**
> If she be not so to me
> What care I how fair she be?
> —Ben Jonson
> (1572–1637)

> If *snow be* white, why then her breast are dun;
>
> If *hairs be* wires, black wires grow on her head.

Today, *snow be* and *hairs be* would be considered odd at best, if not wrong. We tend to use the subjunctive in the twenty-first century for just two reasons:

1. To express a condition contrary to fact:

    If *I were* a wealthy man (but I'm not), I'd fly us to Bali.

    If *he were* arriving tomorrow, we could go to the concert (but he's not coming until next week).

My favorite brand of yogurt used to carry a note on the inner lid that said it tasted just as good as if the owner's mother, Rose, *were* still making it as she had when he was a child. It gave me a happy feeling to see that subjunctive at breakfast—started my day off just right. To my dismay, the copy has changed and now reads "as if Rose *was* making it herself." Sigh. *Sic transit*. Like the canary in the mine, my yogurt carton may herald the eventual demise of the subjunctive. But not yet. Stick with the subjunctive for conditions contrary to fact. It adds a shade of meaning by clearly communicating that something isn't true. As opposed, say, to a simple condition:

> If *Ulrike was coming*, he said he'd arrange to get the day off.

Here's another, as sung by Paul McCartney:

> I would be sad if our new *love was* in vain.

In these cases, the outcome is simply unknown—maybe this will happen, maybe not. In this case, which is *not* contrary to fact, you don't use the subjunctive. If you do, you'll sound like a self-important smarty-pants (like people who say "PROH-cess-eez," which is 100-percent incorrect) to people who know better.

Here's a *past* condition contrary to fact resulting in a mistake:

No: If *he would have told* me (but he didn't), I would have taken him off that bus.

No: If *she would have worked* a full day (which she didn't), I would have paid her for a full day.

It should be simply "If *he had*" and "If *she had*." I think perhaps people mistake the "if...would have..." construction as a subjunctive form. I see and hear it, and I cringe. And I'm not the only one, so please don't do it.

While I'm on the subject, never, ever say *would of*. There is no such construction. It's *would have*. If you're tempted, remember that past tenses are created with the help, if they need help, of the verb *to have*: She has whistled, she had whistled, she will have whistled. *Of*, on the other hand, obviously isn't even a verb.

No (no, no!): If you had asked, I *would of* lent you my hat rack.

Yes: If you had asked, I *would have* lent you my hat rack.

The same goes for *should of*: There is simply no such construction.

2. With requests, suggestions, or demands:

> I *ask* that *you be* dignified and refrain from laughing during the ceremony. I also *ask* that *Shelley refrain* if possible from weeping.
>
> Roger *recommended* that *Larry be* on hand to launch the catboat.
>
> The evil pirate king *commanded* that *Davy walk* the plank.

That's it for the subjunctive these days: for a condition contrary to fact, and with verbs of requesting or demanding.

Try Not to Split the Infinitive Form of a Verb

Some people are frightened by infinitives in the abstract, and I don't blame them. If you don't know what it is, how will you know if you've split one? Happily, there's nothing mysterious about it. Simply put, an infinitive is the *to* form of a verb: *to handle, to help, to wander.* The notion that the two words of an infinitive should not be parted seems to have originated in the 19th century when somebody noticed that in Latin the infinitive is expressed as one word: *amare* (to love), or *esse* (to be). For some reason eager to emulate the construction of a language that had been dead for centuries, influential grammarians proceeded to declare that splitting the infinitive constituted a no-no in English as well.

> **What's the Problem?**
>
> While we're on the subject: Certain words derived from Latin and ending in *is* form plurals by changing the *is* to *es*:
>
> | | |
> |---|---|
> | basis | bases |
> | oasis | oases |
> | thesis | theses |
>
> The plural is pronounced with a long e: *base-eez.* Please note that *process* does not end in *is*. Nobody likes a pseudo-academic, especially one who's wrong.

Here's an example of a split that could actually cause confusion:

> Jerry asked us to more carefully and specifically than in the past plan for a hostile takeover.

It's not nice to fool your readers, and you just might do it with this sentence because the two halves of the infinitive, *to* and *plan*, are so widely separated that someone reading casually could mistake *plan* for a noun. Right? Somebody made a plan in the past for a takeover. That kind of split is worth mending.

That said, many grammatical blunders are worse than a split infinitive, especially when the two halves of the verb aren't widely separated:

> She is inclined *to sharply correct* other people's children.

> It's naïve *to truly believe* in magic.

Experts all agree there's nothing wrong with such little splits, especially in cases where it would be difficult to put the word elsewhere:

> I asked Gina *to simply ignore* the sign for the time being.

To ignore simply the sign? To ignore the sign simply? And *asked Gina simply to ignore* is ambiguous, too: Did I ask her simply, or was the ignoring simple? The sentence works best with *simply* splitting the infinitive, as you'd surely do in conversation.

Now here comes the big *however.* It seems that many people learned the rule about not splitting infinitives. They learned it so well I picture the type of teaching that's accompanied by whacks of the ruler. This makes them very good at identifying splits and thinking less of the people who commit what to them is a huge and yucky error. These people tend to be older and in a position of authority. Do you see where I'm heading with this?

WHY RISK IT?...

She splits her infinitives.

I won't forbid you to split the infinitive, especially in cases such as the examples here, but I will tell you this: I myself absolutely refuse to do it. Why risk offending someone important? This is particularly true when you are writing to a large audience. Who knows who'll read, see the split, and ignore everything you're trying to say?

So I relocate:

> She's inclined to correct other people's children *sharply.*

Or rewrite:

> Some people *truly believe* in magic; I think that's naïve.

Or remove the splitter. Did *simply* really add anything to this sentence?

> I asked Gina to ignore the sign for the time being.

I operate with a simple philosophy: I believe in offending the smallest number of people as infrequently as possible. This informs much of my writing. If enough people think something is an error, I'm not going near it. A cowardly but effective strategy, it works for me and it'll work for you.

Use the Passive Voice Sparingly

Verbs that take objects have two forms, or voices: active and passive. Here's the active voice of a few common verbs:

to do   to have   to eat   to watch

The passive voice is formed by any form of the verb *to be* plus the past tense of the verb:

to be done   to be had   to be eaten   to be watched

Using the passive voice of a verb, we say *It is done, A good time was had, The food will be eaten, The house had been watched.* I'm sure you're familiar with the form.

How do the two voices compare? Which should you use? Let's have a look. Here's a sentence featuring the active voice of the verb *to throw*:

> *Dale threw* a rock through Mrs. James's window yesterday.

The subject is *Dale*. The verb is *threw*.

And here's the same sentence recast in the passive voice:

> *A rock was thrown by Dale* through Mrs. James's window yesterday.

The subject is *A rock*. The verb is *was thrown*.

As you can see, the two sentences are saying pretty much the same thing, but in different ways. Now I will get up on my usual soapbox to declare that in almost all cases it is better to use active verbs rather than passive ones.

What's Wrong With the Passive Voice?

Quite a few things:

1. It takes more words to create a passive construction. *Dale threw a rock* is just four words; *A rock was thrown by Dale* takes six.

2. The passive voice takes most of the action out of the sentence. In our example, the colorful verb form *threw* becomes the participle *thrown*, and the overused, non-action verb *to be* moves in.

3. The object becomes the subject. The real doer of the action, *Dale*, has been pushed deep into the sentence and the object of the verb, *rock*, has become the subject. That further drains action from the sentence.

4. The action goes backward. The result of #3 is that **the sentence runs in reverse**: Instead of subject, verb, and object, which is how sentences typically run, the real subject is last and the object has become the subject, so we have object, verb, and finally subject. Flying in the face of nature? Maybe not quite; but seriously, it isn't great.

5. The subject is allowed to vanish. Note also that, if you wish, you may *remove the original subject* from your sentence altogether:

   A rock was thrown through Mrs. James's window yesterday.

Dale has disappeared from the sentence. Depending on what you're writing, this can make you sound as if you're trying to hide something. Like Dale. In fact, if you care about Dale, you probably are. But it's not attractive, and it's information-poor by contrast with the sentence in the active voice.

For these reasons, the passive form of verbs is generally one to avoid.

Remember: A clue that you're using a passive verb is any form of the verb *to be* paired with a past verb form:

Sushi *cannot be made* with a hacksaw.

You will be seated next to Aunt Roberta.

Ann and Jeffrey loved the prize *they had been given*.

It's usually easy to recast a sentence in the active voice:

You can't make sushi with a hacksaw.

We've seated you next to Aunt Roberta.

Ann and Jeffrey loved the prize *they had won*.

Get in the habit of rewriting when you see a passive verb form in your copy. Once in a while, however, you may want or need to use the passive voice.

Here are three good reasons to prefer passive constructions:

1. When it doesn't matter who did something, or the receiver of the action is more important than the doer.

   > The pope *was praised* for meeting with the victims of abuse.

   We don't care so much who—the media, the Catholic diocese, the faithful—praised the pope. The importance of the sentence lies in the important person who received praise.

   > The flowers *were distributed*, the bridesmaids *were divided* into pairs, the first strains of the organ *were heard*, and the procession began.

   Again, who cares who performed those various operations? Probably three different people, and how tedious it would be to write them in! The passive voice is clearly the right choice here.

2. When the doer is unknown.

   > A package that ticks *was left* in Gertrude's mailbox.

   And we sure hope it's just a clock. We don't know who left it, and we're backing away slowly.

   The passive form is appropriate—in fact, necessary—in such a case.

3. When you wish to avoid blaming yourself or someone else.

   > A mistake *was made* in our classified department, so your ad read, "Snowblower, $10,000" instead of "$100."

   The passive voice can protect a new employee; your spouse, who's terrible at math; or your offspring, who got his learner's permit and took out Mrs. Casey's gatepost.

Bottom line: The passive voice can be a helpful tool in your writing. But these three uses for it notwithstanding, try not to use it if you don't have to. Some people feel it has a nice, businesslike sound. I think it sounds shifty, and I'm not alone. What's wrong with "Jeremy knocked down Mrs. Casey's gatepost and will be spending his allowance for the next four months to have it rebuilt"? Use your judgment.

When you see you've used a passive construction, ask yourself whether it has any excuse for living (see the reasons just mentioned), and, if it doesn't, rewrite to leave it out.

Be Aware of Another Important Aspect of the Verb *To Be*

I suspect you know your way around this verb inside and out, but people are sometimes tripped by one odd facet. In French they say, "C'est moi"—literally, "It's me"—as well as in a number of other languages. But in English, we don't say "It's me." Well, my mother wouldn't let me—I had to respond, "It is I" on the phone if someone asked for me. Just in case your mother wasn't that kind of girl, here's a brief review: The verb *to be* takes the subject case for all pronouns at the far end, where normally an object would go. Here are a few examples:

It was *I* who stole your iPod.

Jesus was *He* whom the wise men were seeking.

Who is responsible? It is *she*.

If these sentences seem to you prim or affected, simply don't use the construction. Write "I stole your iPod," "The wise men were seeking Jesus," and "She is responsible." As for "It is I," it still makes me feel stuffy as a butler to say it, but in my business I can't afford to say "It's me," let alone write it. In all but the most formal conversations, you probably can get away with it, but don't you document it in writing either. Reword, or write "It is I."

Make the Most of Your Verbs

Use Different Verb Tenses to Create Different Effects

I have a pair of tenses in mind:

I expect your report on cryogenic metallurgy by Thursday.

I am expecting your report on cryogenic metallurgy by Thursday.

Notice the difference in tone between those two sentences. One's forceful, and one's gentle. The present tense *I expect* makes a strong statement: We can picture a boss, perhaps, who isn't going to be happy if that report isn't on the rosewood desk

Thursday morning. We could probably add *or else* to the sentence without changing the tone. The *–ing* (a present participle, if you're interested) form produces quite a different impression. Someone thinks the report will probably be done by Thursday— maybe it will, maybe it won't. That's the way *I'm thinking, I'm hoping, I'm asking* come across: In some cases the tense sounds almost tentative. There's nothing tentative about *I think, I hope, I ask*: They create robust statements. Be aware of this in your writing!

Don't Make Nouns Out of Verbs

Take a look at the following list of verb phrases:

to add strength	to have a preference
to be a participant	to do an investigation
to give a performance	to say a prayer

Do you notice anything odd about them? For one thing, each is three or four words long. How did that happen? I'll tell you. In each case, the writer has *backed off,* so to speak, from the real verbs and turned them into nouns! Yes, we've got a frog prince situation here. Each of those last nouns—performance, investigation, and the rest—is a verb in disguise. Just take a look: The hidden verb in each phrase, respectively, is *strengthen, participate, perform, prefer, investigate,* and *pray.*

This "nounifying" isn't something to copy. It isn't incorrect, but it's wordy, and it saps the strength of your sentence. The verbs that have been added are weak little words we barely notice: *to be, to do, to have.* And all the action has been lost: The phrases are static and colorless by contrast with the verbs that have become nouns. Watch out for this unfortunate practice and avoid it in your own writing.

✹ IN BRIEF

> Make sure you know the correct forms for verb tenses.

> When describing an event or experience, don't switch tenses.

> Be sure tenses are in the proper order.

> Don't use the helping verb *did* if *have* works.
> Learn to use the subjunctive mood.
> Try not to split the infinitive form of a verb.
> Use the passive forms of verbs sparingly.
> Be aware of another important aspect of the verb *to be*.
> Make the most of your verbs.

MAKE SURE YOU'VE GOT IT!

Correct the verbs, if necessary, in the following sentences:

1. Did you already buy the Cool Whip for Sandy's Under-the-Sea Salad?
2. Several crucial tax documents were shredded by that miserable Uriah Sweeney.
3. Hunter asked whether I was coming to the rodeo on Saturday.
4. Isn't he planning to quickly return with the winning ticket?
5. I insist that Sherry gives back the coins she stole from the cabinet.
6. He taken his red pickup truck and run over the girls in their tent.
7. If my boss was a sympathetic person, I'd ask, but he's mean as a rattlesnake.
8. Schwartz offered to do an analysis of our business practices.
9. If they be too heavy, just drop those geography books by the dumpster.
10. The annual report was printed, bound, and addressed all in one night.
11. Please let Shipping and Receiving know whether you expect to by the end of this week or at the beginning of the next overnight us those sprockets.
12. Peter couldn't explain what he seen because he knew no one would of believed him.
13. The cleaners have shrank your new trousers: I should of washed them myself.

14. When Mary spoke with her, Susan had told her John lost the house through gambling.

15. The biographer has a tendency to gloss over the difficult areas of his subject's life.

Answer Key

1. *Have you already bought* the Cool Whip for Sandy's Under-the-Sea Salad?

2. *That miserable Uriah Sweeney shredded* several crucial tax documents.

3. Hunter asked whether I was coming to the rodeo on Saturday. CORRECT AS WRITTEN

4. Isn't he planning *to return quickly* with the winning ticket?

5. I insist that Sherry *give back* the coins she stole from the cabinet.

6. He *had taken* his red pickup truck and run over the girls in their tent. OR He *took* his red pickup truck and *ran* over the girls in their tent.

7. If my boss *were* a sympathetic person, I'd ask, but he's mean as a rattlesnake.

8. Schwartz offered *to analyze* our business practices.

9. If they *are* too heavy, just drop those geography books by the dumpster.

10. The annual report was printed, bound, and addressed all in one night. CORRECT AS WRITTEN

11. Please let Shipping and Receiving know *to overnight us those sprockets* by the end of this week or at the beginning of the next.

12. Peter couldn't explain what he *saw* because he knew no one would *have* believed him.

13. The cleaners have *shrunk* your new trousers: I should *have* washed them myself.

14. When Mary spoke with her, Susan *told* her John *had* lost the house through gambling.

15. The biographer *tends* to gloss over the difficult areas of his subject's life.

Pronouns:
A Special Case

Let's look at the pronouns, in case you haven't thought about them as a group lately (or ever).

What are pronouns? They are substitutes for a noun—a person, place, or thing:

> Mary swam; *she* swam.
>
> Justin hit the ball; Justin hit *it*.
>
> This is my house; *it* is *mine*.

Note that the pronouns are really, really old. How old are they? They are so old that they have *endings that change* depending on how they are used in a sentence. The rest of our nouns used to change endings in the same way, as they do in Latin and some other (read "hard") languages. As if English weren't hard enough. Our noun endings don't really change now except to go from singular to plural, thank heaven. So pronouns are all we have left of ancient English—it's like finding a triceratops tailbone. Well, maybe not quite that exciting.

It's important, anyway, to grab the pronoun from the correct column when you write. The chart on page 26 lists the pronouns according to their functions.

Don't be intimidated: After all, you use these pronouns correctly in conversation every day. But it's worth noting which ones fall into which category, because it can save you from making errors in an important piece of writing.

	Subject Case	Object Case	Possessive Case
Singular	I	me	mine
	you	you	yours
	he, she, it	him, her, it	his, hers, its
	who	whom	whose
Plural	we	us	ours
	you	you	yours
	they	them	theirs
	who	whom	whose

(And *this*, *that*, *these*, and *those*, keep the same form no matter how they are used, a fact in which we can all take comfort.)

Make Sure Prepositional Phrase Pronoun Objects Are in the Object Case
(That Is, the Done-To, the Me/Him/Us/Them Case)

The Eighties have a few things to answer for, including women's linebacker shoulder pads and the following lyrics sung by Eric Carmen:

> With these hungry eyes
> One look at you and I can't disguise
> I've got hungry eyes.
> I feel the magic between you and I....

His feelings do him no end of credit, but his grammar—between you and *me*—is lousy because Mr. Carmen's song has a problem with pronoun case. Not content merely with drippy lyrics, the writer of "Hungry Eyes" has committed a grammar gaffe that gives instructors the extra-special yips. It's not "between you and *I*," and it's never going to be. It's "between you and *me*." Here's why.

When you see a preposition—that's one of those words of location, often a little word (*over*, *under*, *of*, *in*, *above*, and so forth)—that's a signal that any pronoun that follows will be in the object category. That's why "between you and I" is incorrect. Forever.

More ungrammatical singing, this time from the Doors back in the day:

> I'm gonna love you till the heavens stop the rain
> And I'm gonna love you till the stars fall from the sky
> For you and I.
> Come on, come on....

Come on is right. For some reason, many people believe that *I* is always more correct than *me*. They think it sounds—oh, I don't know, somehow more formal. Or better educated. They are, of course, wrong in many cases. Unfortunately, it's when people are trying extra hard to be correct that they say or even write "between you and I," "for Jane and I," "about she and I" (yep, the *she* is wrong also). Believe me: This is not the way to impress anyone who knows his or her way around the English language. And such people—your boss, the bank loan officer—are often the very people making decisions about your future.

Interestingly, making this pronoun mistake is unlikely to the vanishing point when there's only one pronoun. Trouble comes when there are two pronouns (*she and I*) or another noun and a pronoun (*the dog and I*). I call this the Phenomenon of the Paired Pronouns. It's with the pairing that errors arise.

Therefore, the easiest way to see for yourself that a pronoun choice is incorrect is to divide the two and use each in your sentence separately. For example:

> Come to McDonald's with *Tony and I.*

Try it. Divide the objects of the "with" clause:

> Come to McDonald's *with Tony.*

> Come to McDonald's *with I.*

You'd never even dream of saying *with I.* It's "Come to McDonald's with Tony and *me.*"

> The CIA agent lived downstairs from *he and she* all summer.

From he? From she? It's easy to see the mistake when you take the pronouns separately. Of course it's *from him and her.*

All Pronouns Standing for Objects Should Also Be in the Object/Done-To Case

When a pronoun is the *object* of a verb—something is being done to a person, place, or thing—it's clear that you should put it in the object case:

I took *her* to the airport that awful Friday when it snowed.

Because this woman is the object of the verb *took*—the writer took her—*her* must be in the object case. Trouble comes—you guessed it—when there's more than one object and at least one pronoun. Uncoupling the two (or more) works here also. Here we go with two objects:

I took *she and Mel* to the airport that awful Friday when it snowed.

Amazing how that happens. Unpair the two objects:

I took *she* to the airport that awful Friday when it snowed.

I took *Mel* to the airport that awful Friday when it snowed.

Your ear instantly tells you that *I took she* is ridiculous. It's *I took her*—look at the chart on page 26—because *her* is in that middle column with the other object pronouns.

A Pronoun Standing for a Subject Must Be in the Subject, or Doer, Case

Subjects usually are the doers or initiators of action. We can use the same "unpairing" technique to see whether we've wrongly substituted an object pronoun for a subject one:

Me and Jennifer want to go to into town so I can return the blue skirt.

Try your subjects separately: You get "*Me wants to go.*" You'd

> ### Are the pronouns in the following sentence right or wrong?
>
> George Willoughby wonders why *his* fiancé didn't invite *he* and *his* mother to the opera, but Geneva and *I* think *it's* because *her* and that family of *her's* are ashamed of the Willoughbys.
>
> Answer: *him* and his mother; *she* and that family; that family of *hers* (The rest are correct.)

never even say that, let alone write it, and you mustn't do it when you have two subjects either. Here's another:

Michael and him don't like that laundromat.

Okay, Michael doesn't like it; but *him* doesn't? You can easily see it's *he*, the pronoun from the subject column.

Unpairing Works Equally Well on Pronouns Standing Directly Beside a Noun

A similar problem can occur with such constructions as this (one of my personal favorites):

Us engineers don't need grammar.

Famous last words. But again, it's the pairing of the words *us* and *engineers* that derailed this hapless writer, who would surely never have said *Us don't need*. It's *We engineers*.

Pronouns and Nouns Must Agree in Number

This isn't hard. It simply means that the pronoun that stands in for a single noun or name must be single as well:

Mary Beth is ill. *She* won't be in today.

The lilacs are out, and *they* are especially beautiful this spring.

Thomas and I are friends: *We* have known each other for years.

Not hard, as I said, but as usual there's a catch. Here's a familiar error:

When a lawyer is disbarred, *they* are not allowed to practice.

This is completely wrong and indefensible. Just because you don't want to say *he* and offend all the women, or *she* and offend all the men, doesn't give you the right to write wrong! I mean incorrectly. Until we come up with a gender-blind pronoun that doesn't sound bizarre, try to work around the problem:

* ❈ Use *you*: You are not allowed to practice law if you have been disbarred.

* ❈ Recast in plural: When lawyers are disbarred, they are not allowed to practice.

* ❈ Rewrite: A disbarred lawyer is not allowed to practice.

I give you some other tips for avoiding disagreements in number in Chapter 7 on agreement. One further thought: I am not wild about using *he or she, him or her, his or her,* or *s/he*. As for alternating *he* and *she*, I think whoever came up with the idea ought to be severely disciplined. Though these devices aren't incorrect, they are distracting. People reading your copy may find their eye drawn to them, even counting them on the way down the page, instead of reading, and you want them to pay attention. So try to limit yourself to one per written piece if you must use them at all.

Look at any decent newspaper or magazine: You won't see a flock of *he or shes* cluttering up the copy. You won't see the grammar error of singular subject and plural pronoun often, either. Believe me: It's not because the problem didn't arise; it's because somebody carefully and defensively wrote around it. Try it. Your readers will like it.

Possessive Pronouns Do NOT Take Apostrophes

It's just a fact. You've probably learned that we usually form possessives by adding an apostrophe with or without an *s*: The boat belonging to Steve is *Steve's boat*. Correct—except for the *possessive* pronouns, the ones in the right-hand column of the chart. They do not ever, ever have an apostrophe anywhere in them. There is therefore absolutely no reason for you to write *her's* or *their's* unless you are writing a linguistics dissertation and are referring to them as words. And that goes double for *it's* unless you mean *it is* or *it has*. Same with *who's*. "*Who's* on first?" Fine. But it's "*Whose* purse is this?"

If you're in doubt as to whether you should write *its* or *it's*, see whether you can substitute *belonging to it*, *it is*, or *it has*:

The yak had somehow gotten out of *its/it's* cage.

Just say to yourself, "The cage belonging to it" and "it is cage." You can easily see that the first phrase represents the meaning you are after, whereas the second is nonsense.

Same with *whose* or *who's*:

She's the only one *whose/who's* got any talent for pole dancing.

"She's the only one *belonging to whom* got any talent?" Nonsense. But "She's the only one *who is/has* got any talent" works:

"One who has got any talent" makes sense. So the correct form is *who's*.

When in doubt, consult your handy pronoun chart, possessive case. If you're writing about a person, place, or thing possessing something, those are your words.

Look Out for *Who* and *Whom*

Many people are tripped up by the difference between *who* and *whom*. I have met students who've told me that they use *whom* in formal writing, otherwise it's always *who*. This makes me want to beat their heads in with a brick. This is English grammar, folks, and you don't get to make up your own rules. Again, a look at the chart clearly shows that *who* is the subject pronoun, the one that is doing whatever's being done: *who wants, who is calling, who swims*.

In contrast, *whom* has its place in the second column. It is the object pronoun, the person, place, or thing that is done to: "I asked her *whom* she was seeing," "*whom* you choose," and of course the excellent memory aid, "*Who* is doing what to *whom*?"

If you're still shaky on this, you can substitute another pronoun—*he* and *him*, for example—for *who* and *whom*, respectively: "*He* is calling," "*him* you choose" (you choose him), "*He* is doing what to *him*?" If *he* is correct, write *who*; if *him* is correct, write *whom*.

Use *None* Correctly

The pronoun *none* can take a singular or a plural verb if it means *not any*. It takes a singular verb if the following noun is singular:

> *None* of his *stamp collection* is at all valuable.

If the following noun is plural, it takes a plural verb:

> *None* of our *children are* coming this Christmas. (We have three. It could have been one, two, or three of them. Therefore *none* here means *not any*; compare with the plumbers example that follows, where *none* means *not a single one*.)

If *none* means *not one*, you should use a singular verb:

> Jim called three plumbers, but *none has* called back. (Not even one!)

Don't Use *Myself* or Any of the Other "Selfs" as a Substitute for Their Simpler Forms

I didn't include these pronouns in the chart because they don't change case. But their misuse is similar to the mistake of my students who think *whom* is just a fancy form of *who*. (Or did, before I got hold of them.) You may have heard or read sentences along these lines:

Abby and *myself* were among the first contestants.

We look forward to meeting George and *yourself*.

Some people have an idea that it is more businesslike to write *myself* and *yourself* instead of plain old *I* and *you*. I urge you respectfully not to join their ranks. You will sound uneducated to the well-informed and self-important to the ignorant.

Once again, if you unpair the noun and pronoun you'll quickly see the *–self* form doesn't work: *Myself was among...*, *to meeting yourself*. Write *Abby and I*, and *George and you*.

Here are the two approved uses of *myself*:

1. As a reflexive (when you are doing something to yourself): I hit *myself*.

2. As an intensifier: He *himself* knew nothing of her other husband.

Same with *herself*, *themselves*, and the rest. Don't risk writing that sounds pompous: To the perceptive reader, that may be even worse than writing incorrectly—a chilling thought.

✹ IN BRIEF

> Make sure prepositional phrase pronoun objects are in the object case (that is, the done-to, the *me/him/us/them* case).

> All pronouns standing for objects should also be in the object/done-to case.

> A pronoun standing for a subject must be in the subject, or doer, case.

> Unpairing works equally well on pronouns standing directly beside a noun.

> Pronouns and nouns must agree in number.

> Possessive pronouns do NOT take apostrophes.

> Look out for *who* and *whom*.

> Use *none* correctly.

> Don't use *myself* or any other "selfs" as a substitute for their simpler forms.

MAKE SURE YOU'VE GOT IT!

Correct any pronoun glitches as necessary in the following sentences:

1. I don't believe its a sin to go cow tipping, and Jerome and me do it all the time.
2. Cousin Edie and myself were the youngest people at the reunion.
3. Mary Jane wonders what sort of powers the children of Spiderman and she will have.
4. I didn't recognize the voice as her's, so I asked whom was calling.
5. Susan and him are just this side of crazy about those boots of your's.
6. None of us are going to Whitney's bridal shower, though she's the one who we like best.
7. The portable GPS, which I think is your's, was a disappointment, but she and Bill made it to the wedding anyway.
8. Whom shall I say is here to see Mrs. Gottrocks?
9. When a captain gives an order, he expects to be obeyed.
10. Can me and Bobby sleep in the van?
11. For us soldiers, there's little choice where we go: The Army makes it's own rules.
12. Between he and John, there's an impractical streak you could drive a truck through.
13. It's a birthday year for LLBean, and they're giving out free lunch coupons in Freeport.

14. Whose coming with Donna and us to pick up Uncle Rick and he at the airport?

15. Us left-handed people put up with a lot of right-handed tools.

16. They want you to sing with Suzanne and I.

Answer Key

1. I don't believe *it's* a sin to go cow tipping, and Jerome and *I* do it all the time.

2. Cousin Edie and *I* were the youngest people at the reunion.

3. Mary Jane wonders what sort of powers the children of Spiderman and *her* will have.

4. I didn't recognize the voice as *hers,* so I asked *who* was calling.

5. Susan and *he* are just this side of crazy about those boots of *yours.*

6. None of us are going to Whitney's bridal shower, though she's the one *whom* we like best.

7. The portable GPS, which I think is *yours,* was a disappointment, but she and Bill made it to the wedding anyway.

8. *Who* shall I say is here to see Mrs. Gottrocks?

9. *A captain who gives* an order expects to be obeyed. OR *When captains give orders, they expect* to be obeyed.

10. Can *Bobby and I* sleep in the van?

11. For us soldiers, there's little choice where we go: The Army makes *its* own rules.

12. Between *him* and John, there's an impractical streak you could drive a truck through.

13. It's a birthday year for LLBean, and *the store is* giving out free lunch coupons in Freeport. OR It's a birthday year for LLBean, and *it is* giving out free lunch coupons in Freeport.

14. *Who's* coming with Donna and us to pick up Uncle Rick and *him* at the airport?

15. *We* left-handed people put up with a lot of right-handed tools.

16. They want you to sing with Suzanne and *me.*

Adjectives:
Colorful! Charming! Correct!

Adjectives add an important dimension to your writing by giving it color and charm. Compare "I saw the man" with "I saw the withered, stooped old man." The adjectives fill in the blanks; they paint a picture; they provide a wealth of information. Of course, it's important to use them correctly as well.

You already know a lot about the way adjectives work. You know that they describe things, which is a normal person's way of saying they modify nouns. If you write *a thrilling spectacle*, *thrilling* is an adjective that tells what kind of *spectacle* you're talking about. If you use too few adjectives, your picture will be incomplete. If you use too many, your writing becomes overloaded and cloying. And of course, this being the kind of book it is, I'm here to tell you can do worse things than that with adjectives. Following are some of the behaviors of adjectives that can lead to errors in writing.

Use the Correct Form of a Compound Adjective

Compound adjectives are adjectives made of more than one word: a *well-intentioned* comment, for example. Compound adjectives may be written in three ways. Some are written open: *reddish violet* crayon; some are written closed: *longtime* friends; some are hyphenated: *cling-free* sheets. Your online or on-shelf dictionary surprisingly often includes these, and the *Chicago Manual of Style* classifies six pages' worth of different kinds of compound words. It's a very helpful guide.

The hyphenated adjectives are the most interesting and cause the most perplexity. Here are two examples of hyphenated adjectives:

In his briefcase was an *almost-finished* novel.

When the leading lady fell ill, the understudy gave an *over-the-top* performance.

Because these adjectives come before their nouns, as you can see, we use hyphens between their parts to avoid any confusion about the relationships between the words. Note that if you write "her performance was over the top," the prepositional phrase *over the top* serves as an adjective, but, because it follows the noun it modifies, there is no need to add hyphens; the meaning is clear. Also, a compound adjective formed by an *-ly* adverb and an adjective—*poorly fitting suit*, *swiftly moving stream*—is not usually hyphenated. Again, the familiar form of the adverb makes the meaning clear. (See Chapter 16 for more than you wanted to know about hyphens.)

Once you've settled on the appropriate form, be consistent. Depending on which dictionary or manual you consult (or the house style if you work for an agency or business), you may find some variations, especially in new words: *logon command*, *log-on command*. Don't worry too much about it; just be consistent in the way you write such adjectives, at least within a piece. Don't write *long term care* in one paragraph and *long-term care* in the next.

When Making Comparisons, Compare Similar Things, Not Apples and Oranges

Adjectives have comparative forms. We say *hot*, *hotter*, *hottest* to describe increasing grades of heat. Comparative adjectives are sometimes irregular, sometimes helped out by adverbs, such as *more* and *much*:

good	better	best
bad	worse	worst
safe	safer	safest
ill	more ill	most ill
interested	much interested	very much interested

Remember to compare two things that match one another. An unbalanced comparison is sloppy, there's no excuse for it, and it makes you look silly. Compare apples to apples. Here's what I mean:

> My biology report is much bigger than my lab partner.

Probably not. I'm guessing this sad person meant to say *much bigger than my lab partner's.*

Unbalanced comparisons are illogical—that is, they don't make sense. How would you fix the following?

> Overfishing in the Pequod River is more serious than Moose Brook.

This says Moose Brook is less serious—you know how those brooks babble. Almost certainly not what the writer intended, but not hard to put right in any of several ways. Here's one suggestion:

> Overfishing in the Pequod River is more serious than in Moose Brook.

You can turn the comparative adjective *more serious* into an adverb:

> The Pequod River has been overfished more seriously than Moose Brook.

In the first correct example, you are now comparing two prepositional phrases: *in the Pequod River* and *in Moose Brook.* In the second, you're comparing nouns: *the Pequod River* and *Moose Brook.* You can see that in both cases the two items match. That's what you want in your own work.

Avoid Half-Finished Comparisons

Don't leave an ungrammatical phrase hanging unfinished in your sentence. Here's what I mean:

> I think my work is *as good if not better* than Beth's, but the manager promoted her.

> Denton Fuller is the quarterback, and the coach thinks he is *as fast if not faster* than Morris Abel, who graduated last year.

In both cases, the correct phrase should be *as...as.* Otherwise that first comparison is actually saying *as good than Beth's if not better than Beth's.* The second says *he is as fast than Morris, if not faster.* Neither will win you any points.

While we're at it, if you are writing a comparison, don't stop until you've clarified "compared to what?" Don't simply say that something is *better*, but *better than what*? Advertising freely tells you that this airline will fly you farther, that that outfit will make you sexier, and that such-and-such a product is just plain better. Our eyes and ears are so used to it that we may not recognize it as a half-baked piece of work. Nonetheless, you should if at all possible avoid the half-finished by saying better, farther, and more attractive *than what*.

> **What's the Problem?**
> Poodles are as smart if not smarter than German Shepherds.
>
> Answer: Poodles are as smart AS if not smarter than German Shepherds.

Our new tank tops will make you *sexier than Madonna*.

Our airline flies *farther than any of our competitors*.

Our new turnip twaddler is *better than sliced bread*!

Once you get used to it, you'll almost always create a better sentence. Whoops—I mean better than the original.

Don't Modify Super-Strong Adjectives

Some adjectives are so strong that they should not be modified. *Unique* is a good example of what I mean. Either it's unique or it isn't: Don't say something is *rather unique* or *very unique*. Sometimes a modifier doesn't work: *very principal*? Here are a few you shouldn't modify:

absolute	deadly	preferable
all-powerful	ideal	terminal
complete	immovable	total
critical	massive	utter
	perfect	

And the jury's still out on *pregnant*. Can you be just *a little pregnant*? Some women assert that if you are pregnant with triplets and have gained 60 pounds, you are surely *more pregnant* than the average mom-to-be. I think I'll leave that one right there.

I could list many more of these powerful or absolute adjectives, but I'm guessing you get the idea.

Observe the Rule for Adjectives Ending in *Like*

Here's something tiny but nice to know. Typically, adjectives that end in *like*, such as *dog-like* or *starlike*, are spelled as one word. If the root word ends in two l's, however, you need to put in a hyphen: *bell-like, doll-like*. Otherwise, you'd have three l's in a row, and your word would look like a capital in Eastern Europe. *Belllike?*

Place Adjectives as Close as Possible to the Words They Are Describing

I've said it elsewhere, and it's true here as well: location, location, location. We are physical beings and we are sensitive to placement, tending to believe that things clustered together belong together. Therefore, do not write the following:

Silly or brilliant, I thought we needed to try his suggestion.

You could build a case for a dual-personality narrator—the sentence says *the writer* is silly or brilliant. Put the descriptive words right next to what they describe:

I thought we needed to try his suggestion, silly or brilliant.

Here's another similar goof, this time with a prepositional phrase that serves as an adjective, but describes the wrong noun:

Tyler has bought the little house across from the football field where I was born.

Accidents happen, of course, but this writer was probably born in the little house, not on the football field.

Why is it poor writing? In English, as in many other languages, parts of a sentence that are placed close together appear to be related. It's the placement of *where I was born* directly after *the football field* that makes it look as if the writer were born on the field. Put things that belong together close together. This works a lot, maybe even most, of the time:

> Tyler has bought the little house where I was born, across from the football field.

> Tyler has bought the little house across from the football field.
> It's the house where I was born.

A word in general here: You can't afford to misplace words or phrases. You come off sounding kind of weird. Your reader then brands you as untrustworthy, and as a result mistrusts whatever point(s) you're trying to make.

Use Adjectives, Not Adverbs, to Modify Some Verbs Relating to Being or Seeming

The same goes for sensory verbs: look, sound, taste, smell—and feel, as it relates to health. We write that something is good, looks funny, tastes yummy, and so forth. Don't write that he looked *wonderfully* unless you mean his eyesight was marvelous. *He looked wonderful* is correct. Likewise:

> My new speakers sound *poorly* to me.

No. Your speakers sound poor, bad, even terrible. Back to Circuit City.

Finally, come to terms with the "health issue": Almost all words describing physical and mental health are adjectives: *I feel good about myself, I feel exhausted, I am nauseated. Well* is the exception: The word, usually an adverb (he played well), is used here as an adjective, as in *a well woman*. Note that *I feel badly* means, just as you probably suspect, that your fingers are numb. Compare *I feel horrible*. You wouldn't use the adverb *horribly* to describe your state of health, so don't write *feel badly*.

See Chapter 17 on commas for punctuation of adjectives in a series.

That just about does it for adjective pitfalls. I'm betting you're pretty good at these. If some of them are unfamiliar, read up intensely.

✹ IN BRIEF

> ≫ Use the correct form of a compound adjective.

> ≫ When making comparisons, compare similar things, not apples and oranges.

> ≫ Avoid half-finished comparisons.

> ≫ Don't modify super-strong adjectives.

> ≫ Observe the rule for adjectives ending in *like*.

> ≫ Place adjectives as close as possible to the words they are describing.

> ≫ Use adjectives, not adverbs, to modify some verbs relating to being or seeming.

MAKE SURE YOU'VE GOT IT!

Correct adjective mistakes in the following sentences if necessary.

1. I feel so badly for the poor girl whose Miss America crown was taken away.
2. I think this lava lamp is sort of unique, don't you?
3. The Rockettes' routines are somehow crisper and more energized.
4. East Overshoe Bank has been forced to foreclose on some short-term loans, and we are offering very few short term loans at this time.
5. Brendan was aghast to see celllike mutations in the petri dish.
6. Cecil, our little Houdini, can hold his breath for as long or longer than two minutes.
7. That hamster in the compost pile smells pretty badly: We should bury it.

8. What is this strange and evil sounding rite, Spring Break, of which you speak?

9. As the stunningly-beautiful bridesmaid preceded my bride down the aisle, I thought, Good Lord, I have made the most-horrible mistake.

10. No one speaks even half-decent English here, and I speak Croatian abominably.

11. Yellow with jaundice, Sarah took the baby to the clinic.

12. Though it tasted deliciously, the dessert was too heavy.

13. We need a lawyer: The problem is very desperate.

Answer Key

1. I feel so ***bad*** for the poor girl whose Miss America crown was taken away.

2. I think this lava lamp is ***unique,*** don't you?

3. The Rockettes' routines are somehow crisper and more energized ***than their competitors'.***

4. East Overshoe Bank has been forced to foreclose on some short-term loans, and we are offering very few ***short-term*** loans at this time.

5. Brendan was aghast to see ***cell-like*** mutations in the petri dish.

6. Cecil, our little Houdini, can hold his breath for ***as long as*** or longer than two minutes.

7. That hamster in the compost pile smells pretty ***bad***: We should bury it.

8. What is this strange and ***evil-sounding*** rite, Spring Break, of which you speak?

9. As the ***stunningly beautiful*** bridesmaid preceded my bride down the aisle, I thought, Good Lord, I have made the ***most horrible*** mistake.

10. No one speaks even half-decent English here, and I speak Croatian abominably. CORRECT AS WRITTEN

11. Sarah took the baby, ***yellow with jaundice,*** to the clinic.

12. Though it tasted ***delicious,*** the dessert was too heavy.

13. We need a lawyer: The problem is ***desperate.***

Adverbs: The 4 H Club

Adverbs describe the four h's. I'm referring to *how*, *where*, *why*, and to *what* degree. Sorry, but I'm trying to be memorable here. And isn't it true that those three "w" words are actually pronounced *hwere*, *hwy*, and *hwat*?

I don't plan to spend a lot of your time worrying over adverbs, because I'm guessing you don't have much trouble using them. As with all other parts of English language, though, errors can creep in and give you an amateur-writer label you don't want. So first, let's remind ourselves what adverbs are.

Adverbs Tell How, Where, Why, or to What Degree

They often end in *-ly*. For example:

immediately	aptly
thankfully	mostly
	impressively

Many words that do not end in *-ly* may also be used as adverbs. Here are a few:

very	more, most
hard	ever
how	quite
when	best
	well

Some of these are used as adjectives, which describe nouns, as well.

> FYI: Not every word that ends in -ly is an adverb! All of the following are used to describe people, places, or things—that is, they are nouns, and we know adverbs *don't* describe nouns. They describe verbs, adjectives, or other adverbs. Although they end in -ly, the following are all adjectives:
>
> cowardly   the *Cowardly* Lion
>
> homely   *homely* as a mud fence
>
> leisurely   a *leisurely* cruise (can be an adverb as well)
>
> scholarly   a *scholarly* debate
>
> ghastly   a *ghastly* phantom

Adverbs Can Modify, or Describe, Verbs, Adjectives, or Other Adverbs

❈ Adverbs describing (or modifying) verbs:

I followed her mother and *quickly explained* the situation.

Dick *has impressed* all the stockholders *positively*.

How did you find all these trilobites?

❈ Adverbs describing adjectives:

The sailing conditions in Puget Sound are *constantly changing*.

We saw some *fantastically intricate* Fabergé eggs in St. Petersburg.

I think the story of Princess Diana is *terribly sad*.

❈ Adverbs describing other adverbs:

The slow runners were *very quickly* eliminated.

A steady stream of customers kept us *most busily* occupied.

Austin works *terribly hard* at his construction business.

A Prepositional Phrase Can Be an Adverb

In the sentence *The boy hopped over the fence*, the phrase *over the fence* tells where, describing *hopped*. Here are a few more:

The dark lake was beautiful *in a sinister way*. (describes *beautiful*)

The thief ran *around the corner* and vanished. (tells where he ran)

I go to McDonald's *for breakfast* when I'm feeling glum. (tells why)

Compound Words and Adverbs Ending in *-ly* Generally Don't Require a Hyphen

The hyphen isn't needed because the familiar form of an *-ly* adverb alerts a reader to its function in the sentence.

> a *quickly moving* train
>
> *smoothly flowing* speech
>
> *neatly folded* napkins

Adverbs Not Ending in *-ly* May Cause Confusion if They're Part of Compounds Preceding the Noun They Describe

The pair of words should be hyphenated in this position. That's a complicated way of describing this:

> the *always-popular songs* of Neil Diamond (adverb+adjective+noun)
>
> the *still-scantily clad dancer* (adverb+adverb+adjective+noun)

Without a hyphen, for example, the second fragment could mean the dancer was both still and scantily clad. Not that it matters much, but we're striving for utter clarity here.

The same pair coming *after* the noun can be left as two words, because they aren't going to confuse anyone:

> Neil Diamond's "Sweet Caroline" is always popular at open-mike night.

The dancer was still scantily clad.

NOTE: A hyphen is never wrong, before an *-ly* adverb or elsewhere, if it's needed to clarify meaning. A friend tells me her father used to puzzle people with this sentence:

He had a feebly growing down on his chin.

What on earth is a feebly? Hyphenate after the *-ly* word and the sentence makes sense. Hint: *Down* is a noun here.

I know you're waiting for the other shoe to drop: Where does adverb trouble come in? I don't intend to disappoint you. Please take the following directives to heart.

Be Certain You've Got a Legitimate Adverb to Modify, or Describe, Your Adjective, Adverb, or Verb—Not an Adjective

No: She's *real talented* as a ventriloquist.

Yes: She's *really talented* as a ventriloquist.

No: I suspect he *talks poor* because he *thinks poor*.

Yes: I suspect he *talks poorly* because he *thinks poorly*.

Why are these wrong? Because *real* and *poor* are adjectives, meant to describe nouns: a *real* blessing, a *poor* excuse. Don't use them as adverbs, except in the most informal conversation—maybe with your mother, and I hope she corrects you.

The adjective *slow* is permitted by some dictionaries as an adverb in informal speech or writing. I suggest that you not use it in that way, at least in your writing.

No: We drove the car *slow* so as not to be early to Lurleen's barbecue.

Yes: We drove the car *slowly* so as not to be early to Lurleen's barbecue.

Question Whether an Adverb Such as *Really* or *Very* Strengthens Your Sentence

Be sparing with these. Sprinkling your writing with such intensifiers may in fact weaken your writing:

No: I think Theresa is *really* lovely in her bridesmaid's dress.

Yes: Theresa is lovely in her bridesmaid's dress.

No: Try this book on the five senses. I think you'll find it *very* interesting.

Yes: Try this book on the five senses. I think you'll find it interesting.

The sentences stand without the adverbs and sound just as good as or better than those with the qualifying adverbs. As we discussed in the preceding chapter, be especially careful not to modify a strong adjective.

I find those pedestrian icons with no hands or feet *very ghastly*.

Renee realized she had made an *awfully dreadful* mistake.

You can, believe it or not, make these sentences sound even worse with *minimizing* adverbs.

I find those pedestrian icons with no hands or feet *slightly ghastly*.

Renee realized she had made a *somewhat dreadful* mistake.

The bottom line is that strong adjectives don't *need* adverbs to describe them. They can stand alone, and they should. Don't make yourself ridiculous by embellishing them.

Be Sure Your Adverbs Don't Wander

As with so many words, location of adverbs is important. A rule that works virtually all the time is to ask yourself what the adverb is describing and stick it as close to that word as possible. Otherwise you get some odd effects. Here's what I mean:

These flowers *only* bloom for a day.

The location of the *only* makes the sentence mean that the flowers do nothing but bloom, prompting one to wonder what else they could do. Karaoke? What the *only* is supposed to focus on is the single-day, not the blooming, aspect. Try instead:

These flowers bloom *only* for a day

OR

These flowers bloom for one day *only*.

Only tends to wander particularly badly. Here are a few more examples:

She was *only* a woman with one goal in mind: med school. (only one goal)

Advanced streaming radio *only* plays music you love! (plays only)

If you *only* need to stop at the house for a moment, I'll take you. (only for a moment)

Remember that the position of *only* can make a big difference in the meaning of your sentence. And it may not be obvious to you that you're putting the emphasis in the wrong place, because *you* know what you're trying to say. Here are two sentences that mean quite different things thanks to the different positions of *only*:

Marie offered *only* to pick him up on Fridays. (She was offering chauffeur service but nothing else. She wasn't going to bring lunch.)

Marie offered to pick him up on Fridays *only*. (The other days he'll have to walk.)

Only might be among the worst offenders, but it's not alone. Watch other adverbs that tend to wander as well:

No: I *almost* swam 15 miles when I was training for the Iron Man.

Yes: I swam *almost* 15 miles when I was training for the Iron Man.

In the first sentence, taken literally, our writer didn't actually swim at all. Perhaps he or she went to the dock intending to swim 15 miles and was frightened by a fish. *Almost* tries to modify or describe the word that directly follows it.

No: What are you *still* doing here? (I hate it when someone says that. Way off.)

Yes: What are you doing *still* here?

Better: Why are you *still* here?

Adverb placement can render fine shades of meaning. Compare the following:

> I *just* want you to eat the crackers in the opened box.

That's all I want. You know what I'm saying?

> I want you *just* to eat the crackers in the opened box.

Just eat them. Don't offer them to the folks in the living room.

> I want you to eat *just* the crackers in the opened box.

Leave that unopened box alone or else.

And compare:

> She *still* says she wants to play Ophelia in *Hamlet*.

> She says she *still* wants to play Ophelia in *Hamlet*.

In the first sentence, our leading lady keeps on saying she wants the role of Ophelia. In the second, despite something that has happened—she broke her arm, the director was horrible to her—she *wants* the role.

You can actually achieve some bizarre effects by misplacing adverb phrases:

> I learned that rock superstar Kurt Cobain had died *on CBS*.

It sounds like a demise in front of millions. In fact, our writer meant to say:

> I learned *on CBS* that rock superstar Kurt Cobain had died.

Once again, it's all about location.

On the subject of location, occasionally people get the bit between their teeth and complain that you must not interrupt parts of a verb with an adverb. This is probably an extension of the idea that you shouldn't split an infinitive, such as *to want*: *to* really *want*. So now they don't want you to say "I have *never* fallen down so hard in my life." So what's it going to be, self-styled experts?

I *never* have fallen down so hard. (stilted)

I have fallen down *never* so hard. (unclear; maybe even Olde Englishe)

I have fallen *never* down so hard. (frankly not any kind of Englishe)

Believe me, it is much better to write

He will *clearly* prove himself a
valuable member of the relay team.

than

He *clearly* will prove himself a
valuable member of the relay team.

OR

He will prove himself *clearly* a
valuable member of the relay team.

> **What's the Problem?**
>
> Whether it's with adverbs or anything else, be careful of writing in a stilted or artificial manner. Your readers may think you are trying to act superior to them. You want to avoid this at all costs, because it puts you and your readers at odds. You want them to like you *and*, of course, your message.

The second and third examples sound forced, and, worse still, seem to miss the meaning of the original, which is focused on *prove*. Nowhere is it written, at least not on the huge bookshelf of writing manuals above my computer, that you may not split up the parts of a compound verb. Don't give it another thought.

Don't forget the versatility and usefulness of adverbs. They can buff up your writing as you work to communicate accurately and effectively.

✸ IN BRIEF

> Adverbs tell how, where, why, or to what degree.

> Adverbs can modify, or describe, verbs, adjectives, or other adverbs.

≫ A prepositional phrase can be an adverb.

≫ Compound words and adverbs ending in -ly generally don't require a hyphen.

≫ Adverbs not end ing in -ly may cause confusion if they're part of compounds preceding the noun they describe.

≫ Be certain you've got a legitimate adverb to modify, or describe, your adjective, adverb, or verb—not an adjective.

≫ Question whether an adverb such as *really* or *very* strengthens your sentence.

≫ Be sure your adverbs don't wander.

MAKE SURE YOU'VE GOT IT!

Correct whatever's wrong with these sentences. (Hint: Adverbs may be involved.)

1. In Uncle Tom's Cabin, Simon Legree really embodied evil.
2. It seems to me that Charles is a peacefully happily baby.
3. Beth nearly walked 20 miles for the cancer benefit.
4. Julian behaved cowardly when Angela dared him to jump.
5. As the water poured in, I reflected that our situation was somewhat desperate.
6. As I rocked gently, I wished Jacob had mowed the lawn in the boat.
7. I can only give you a good grade if you write an excellent term paper.
8. No one could seem to persuade the still present man to talk to us.
9. Why is American Express giving a discount if we only pay promptly?
10. He answered niggardly that he couldn't afford to donate $12.
11. Do you think he totally has lost his mind?
12. Her quite unhealthy lifestyle will catch up eventually with her.
13. Her lifestyle seems to me quite-unhealthy.

14. Can you teach me how to dance real slow?

15. He explained the evolution of the word *paradigm* since 1900 very scholarly.

16. You just don't need the size 4 needles; you need 2s and 8s also.

Answer Key

1. In *Uncle Tom's Cabin*, Simon Legree ***embodied*** evil.

2. It seems to me that Charles is a ***peaceful, happy*** baby.

3. Beth walked ***nearly*** 20 miles for the cancer benefit.

4. Julian behaved ***in a cowardly manner*** when Angela dared him to jump.

5. As the water poured in, I reflected that our situation was ***desperate***.

6. As I rocked gently ***in the boat,*** I wished Jacob had mowed the lawn.

7. I can give you a good grade ***only*** if you write an excellent term paper.

8. No one could seem to persuade the ***still-present*** man to talk to us.

9. Why is American Express giving a discount ***only*** if we pay promptly?

10. He answered ***in a niggardly way*** that he couldn't afford to donate $12.

11. Do you think he has ***totally*** lost his mind?

12. Her ***quite-unhealthy*** lifestyle will catch up eventually with her.

13. Her lifestyle seems to me ***quite unhealthy.***

14. Can you teach me how to dance ***really slowly***?

15. He explained the evolution of the word ***paradigm*** since 1900 ***in a scholarly way.*** OR ***His explanation of*** the word ***paradigm*** since 1900 was scholarly.

16. You don't need ***just*** the size 4 needles; you need 2s and 8s also.

✳ 51

Conjunctions:
Strings for Pearls

Just as thread connects the pearls on a necklace, conjunctions connect thoughts within and sometimes between sentences. Like that thread, they are critical to the success of your piece: You'd have no necklace if there were no string—just a pretty but disjointed handful of pearls. Here are some of the most common conjunctions:

and	but	nor	so	though	where	until
although	for	or	that	when	which	yet

Conjunctions make your writing flow smoothly and highlight the relationships between ideas. If conjunctions didn't exist, it would be hard to understand how these separate sentences fit together:

The ship was heavily plated with steel.
The ice was 20 feet thick.
The bow was reinforced and fitted with an ice cutter.
The ship could make no headway.

Throw in a few decent conjunctions, and it's easy to see what the writer is trying to say.

The ship was heavily plated with steel, but the ice was 20 feet thick, so, although the bow was reinforced and fitted with an ice cutter, the ship could make no headway.

If a Conjunction Connects Independent Sentences, Include a Comma Before the Conjunction

The conjunctions that are able to do this I call extra-strength conjunctions. They include:

and   nor   (al)though   or   but   so   for

When using these with two complete sentences, put a comma between them. You may do this so automatically you've never thought about it:

> Johnson stole from the store for years, but nobody caught him.
>
> Mavis had brought a fresh turkey, and she cooked it on the Weber grill.
>
> Dora arrived for her yoga class at 11:30, although she had had no breakfast.

In the previous pairs of joined sentences, each half has a subject and a verb.

If the second half doesn't have its own subject, don't put a comma before the conjunction.

> Vince said he was thirsty and grabbed my Coke before I could object.
>
> I'm not driving four hours to watch Pelvis Wretchley writhe around on stage or waiting backstage for an autograph afterward.

If the sentence pairs are very short and/or closely related in thought, you can omit the comma and the ceiling probably won't fall in.

> Get all A's *and* I'll buy you dinner at Friday's.
>
> He asked for it *so* I punched him.

If two halves of a sentence joined by a conjunction strongly contradict each other, use a comma even if the second part is not a complete sentence on its own.

> It was the UPS guy, not Godot.
>
> Armistead Maupin didn't write *A Tale of Two Cities*, but *Tales of the City*.

Don't Create a Run-On Sentence by Omitting a Conjunction Joining Independent Sentences

Here's what I mean:

No: Bennett had been caught stealing food, the other campers distrusted him.

Yes: Bennett had been caught stealing food, so the other campers distrusted him.

No: You can lead a horse to water, you can't make him drink.

Yes: You can lead a horse to water, but you can't make him drink.

Some conjunctions come in pairs:

both	➡	and
neither	➡	nor
either	➡	or
not only	➡	but also

Be sure, when you use these or others like them, that you put them in parallel positions.

No: She was *not only* his wife, *but also* she was his second cousin.

Yes: She was *not only* his wife, *but also* his second cousin. (*wife* parallels *cousin*)

Yes: *Not only* was she his wife, *but* she was his second cousin *also*. (verbs parallel)

Don't Describe or Explain Something by Using *Is When* or *Is Where*

I had a teacher in grade school who used to give us, as an unpleasant example of this error, "A boy is when he runs." Funny how these things stick with you. She'd be proud to know that

"TORTICOLLIS - O'CLOCK"

"Torticollis, or wry neck, is when the head is tilted toward one side."

at least one of her students was paying attention.

No: Torticollis, or wry neck, *is when* the head is tilted toward one side.

Yes: Torticollis, or wry neck, is a condition in which the head is tilted toward one side

No: The best part *is where* she says, "It's not a man, Daddy."

Yes: The best part is her line "It's not a man, Daddy."

Observe the Difference Between *Which* and *That*

The house which or *the house that*? And you thought they were interchangeable. I wish, but of course it's more complicated than that. Briefly put, which introduces a nonrestrictive clause or adds information.

> This first edition of Dickens's *Oliver Twist*, *which* my aunt found in her attic, is worth quite a lot of money.

That, on the other hand, introduces a restrictive, or defining, clause.

> The box *that* I saw is gone.

I'm happy to mention that H.W. Fowler, in his classic volume, *Modern English Usage*, devoted no fewer than seven—count 'em, seven—pages to the issue of which and that. It makes the following comparatively short explanation look good.

So are you supposed to write *the movie which* or *the movie that*? Not surprisingly, the answer is, it depends.

Use *which* before information that adds facts—perhaps important facts, but facts the sentence can stand alone without.

> The 2007 movie about Edith Piaf, *which* we saw on DVD, is wonderful.

> We paid a visit to the Bull and Finch pub, *which* made me feel like a tourist.

Note that if you remove the two *which* clauses, those two sentences make sense without them. That's because the subject of each clause, the movie and the pub, has already been identified in the first part of the sentence. The *which* clause adds an important fact; still, the sentence can stand alone without it.

(Incidentally, don't forget that clauses come bracketed by *pairs* of commas unless they begin or end your sentence.)

You need to use a *that* clause, on the other hand, when you cannot omit the clause without losing information that identifies the subject and is crucial to the sense of your sentence.

> The convertible *that* my uncle left me is in perfect condition.

> The production of *Cats that* you saw toured southern Italy last season.

The information in the *that* clauses in each case cannot be left out because it answers the questions, respectively, "What convertible?" and "What production?" Remove them and you're left with the following:

> The convertible is in perfect condition.
>
> The production of *Cats* toured southern Italy last season.

You couldn't, for example, initiate an e-mail chat with a friend with either of these sentences. In each case your friend would have no means of identifying either subject: each sentence would just come out of the blue. Again: What convertible? What production? The sentences can't stand on their own in terms of making sense.

Does this seem hard? Allow me to present two surefire ways to tell which of the two words you should use before a given clause. Drum roll, please:

1. If it's an add-a-fact or *which* clause, there will be a comma before the *which*.

2. If it's an essential or *that* clause, if you walk into a room and recite the sentence without the clause, people will think you're weird. If they won't think you're weird, it's *which*.

Try these out on the following sentence. Does *which* or *that* go in the blank?

> Everyone seems to like the James Patterson book *Double Cross* _____ John admired.

Which and a comma? Or *that* and no comma?

> Everyone seems to like the James Patterson book *Double Cross, which* John admired.

> Everyone seems to like the James Patterson book *Double Cross that* John admired.

Well, the first sentence looks all right. The clause "which...admired" adds a "by the way" fact that could be left out, and you could start off a conversation without it without raising eyebrows: "Everyone seems to like the James Patterson book *Double Cross*."

The second sentence—not so much. Because the book is already identified, by author and title, this clause indicates that a number of copies of *Double Cross* are floating around the house, but the one—**that** one—that John admired belongs to the speaker/writer. Or worse, that James Patterson wrote more than one book with that title. Unlikely at best. *Which* is correct.

Here's another:

What is the song _____Madonna sings about an island?

Try which with a comma:

What is the song, *which* Madonna sings about an island?

Remember: By definition *which* introduces a clause that could be left out, leaving you a sentence you could walk into the living room and say and no one would think you're bizarre. Try leaving out "which Madonna sings."

What is the song about an island?

Uh oh. Now try *that*:

What is the song *that* Madonna sings about an island?

Now you're talking. You cannot leave the clause out: it identifies what song you're talking about. *That* and no comma is correct.

Incidentally, because *that* and the rest of the clause are essential to the integrity of the sentence, you can in many cases (though not always) leave *that* out entirely without harm to the sentence.

What is the song Madonna sings about an island?

Accordingly, if you can omit the word, the word should be *that*.

So maybe that was more about *which* and *that* than anybody needed: it's worth it to spell it out, because grammar is all about being right. I promise not to mention it again.

✳ IN BRIEF

> If a conjunction connects two independent sentences, include a comma before the conjunction.

> Don't create a run-on sentence by omitting a conjunction joining two independent sentences.

> Don't describe or explain something by using *is when* or *is where*.

> Observe the difference between *which* and *that*.

MAKE SURE YOU'VE GOT IT!

Correct the use of conjunctions and punctuation, if necessary, in the following sentences.

1. I know it sounds crazy but I'm planning to go back to college.
2. I enjoy YouTube movie reviews which always include video clips taken from the films.
3. Raynaud's syndrome is when your fingers turn yellow in the cold.
4. I belong to a spirituality book club, and am enjoying the books, and the discussions.
5. Jan forgot to bill National Stay Company for the widgets but is sure they'll pay eventually.
6. I have an idea, that I think you will like.
7. Gina wants to book two rooms for the wedding, which is fine with me.
8. Rivers is being eyed for the coaching job, but is refusing to discuss the matter.
9. He seemed to be alone at the bar so I went over and spoke to him.
10. Fran is one of eight women that are running for a seat in the Virginia House of Delegates.
11. She could neither sing nor could she act which effectively put her out of the running.
12. Jennifer asked Paul Yu to be her escort for he was familiar with the St. Regis Hotel.
13. Ask me no questions, I'll tell you no lies.
14. Don't forget to bring a warm coat, Boston is unbelievably cold and raw in March.
15. Some people don't use phone books at all which is surprising to me.

16. Give me $5,000 and a ticket to Portland or I'll tell everyone you lied about the cake.

Answer Key

1. I know it sounds *crazy*, but I'm planning to go back to college.

2. I enjoy YouTube movie *reviews*, which always include video clips taken from the films.

3. Raynaud's syndrome *causes* your fingers *to* turn yellow in the cold.

4. I belong to a spirituality book *club* and am enjoying the books, and the discussions.

5. Jan forgot to bill National Stay Company for the widgets but is sure they'll pay eventually. CORRECT AS WRITTEN

6. I have an *idea* that I think you will like.

7. Gina wants to book two rooms for the wedding, which is fine with me. CORRECT AS WRITTEN

8. Rivers is being eyed for the coaching *job* but is refusing to discuss the matter.

9. He seemed to be alone at the *bar*, so I went over and spoke to him.

10. Fran is one of eight women that are running for a seat in the Virginia House of Delegates. CORRECT AS WRITTEN

11. She could neither sing *nor act*, which effectively put her out of the running.

12. Jennifer asked Paul Yu to be her *escort*, for he was familiar with the St. Regis Hotel.

13. Ask me no questions, I'll tell you no lies. CORRECT AS WRITTEN (BECAUSE THE TWO HALVES ARE SO CLOSELY RELATED)

14. Don't forget to bring a warm coat, *as* Boston is unbelievably cold and raw in March.

15. Some people don't use phone books at *all*, which is surprising to me.

16. Give me $5,000 and a ticket to *Portland*, or I'll tell everyone you lied about the cake.

6

Prepositions:
Location, Location, Location

You do know what a preposition is, whether you think you do or not. You use hundreds of them every day in your conversation and your writing. Prepositions are those words, often little ones, that introduce an explanation of under what circumstances something in a sentence is happening. Often they are words referring to location, and, as any real estate broker can tell you, that's really important. In the following sentence, *by* is a preposition that leads off the prepositional phrase *by the beach*, which in this case tells where Miriam's house is.

Miriam has a little house *by* the beach.

A few of our most common prepositions include:

among	behind	for	on	to
around	between	in	out	under
as	beside	into	over	with
before	by	of	through	without

There are many, many more. Some prepositions are a couple of words long:

apart from   as much as   as regards   instead of

Prepositions are most often found as part of prepositional phrases:

for your sake   over the wall   in the soup   as regards your brother's will

The preposition *to* is ubiquitous as half of a verb infinitive: *to wish, to speak.*

And I wouldn't care whether you know what a preposition or a prepositional phrase is or not except that errors can crop up when you're using them.

For starters, people sometimes make mistakes with the object of a preposition. Here are some prepositions with their objects:

> Identify the prepositions in the following sentence.
>
> I'd go over the river and through the woods for a taste of Grandmother's pudding.
>
> Answer: over, through for, of

to the river	*without* any preparation	*beside* the bed
at the appointed hour	*over* time	*out* the window

Rule: If the object of a preposition is a pronoun, it must be in the object (done-to) case. Here are some examples:

> beside *me*   over *them*   without *you*   through *her*

Errors most often occur when there's more than one object of a preposition:

> In spite of *Darcy and he*, the evening was not a success.
>
> Through the efforts of *I and Josiah*, the company seems to be turning the corner.

Take the two parts of the object apart and the correct pronoun case is quite clear:

> In spite of Darcy; in spite of *he* (No way!)
>
> Through the efforts of *I*; through the efforts of Josiah

Just as you'd never write "the efforts of I," you mustn't write "the efforts of I and Josiah."

The Phenomenon of the Paired Pronouns is discussed more fully in Chapter 2.

Place a Prepositional Phrase as Close as Possible to What It's Describing

Don't, for example, write the following:

> Whom did I see this morning who died *in the newspaper?*

Such stream-of-consciousness prose (following one's train of thought in print) is bad enough in conversation, much worse when documented in writing. Try a rewrite:

Whose obituary did I see in the newspaper this morning?

Be Aware of Placing a Preposition at the End of a Sentence

I'm not saying you should never do it. Many of us learned, for what reason I know not, that you must not end a sentence with a preposition, known as a *terminal preposition* (as if it might kill you). No one seems sure how this got started—some people blame 17th-century dramatist John Dryden—but let me assure you, there are a lot of worse things: writing in a stilted manner, for example. Which sounds better?

My daughter has nothing *to be ashamed of*.

My daughter has nothing *of which to be ashamed*.

The second version, though correct, sounds forced and artificial by comparison with the first, which is the way real people express themselves—usually a good test. Sometimes, in fact, there is no way to avoid ending with a preposition.

As a performer at parties, he was much sought *after*.

Hang up your hat. That's what the hat rack is there *for*.

What are you talking *about*?

Here's Barack Obama on the subject of his former pastor, Jeremiah Wright:

[He was speaking] in terms that people might be taken aback by.

You can't just relocate *by*—you need to rewrite the whole sentence:

[He was speaking] in terms that might take people aback.

However, it may be a wise defense to eliminate ending prepositions if you happen to be writing to someone who's a real stickler for grammar or if you're writing to person(s) unknown. Why risk annoying a reader?

My daughter has no reason to feel ashamed.

As a performer at parties, he was much in demand.

Hang up your hat. That's why we have a hat rack.

Omit Prepositions if Your Meaning Remains Clear

In ordinary usage, prepositions are sometimes skipped:

I am certain David did it *the same way*. [instead of *in the same way*]

If you're going *the same time*, may I ride with you? [instead of *at the same time*]

You may certainly do this as long as the meaning of your sentence remains clear. But sometimes omitting a preposition can result in fuzzy writing.

Not great: I never *tired seeing* the dances of the Masai coming-of-age ceremony.

Better: I never *tired of seeing* the dances of the Masai coming-of-age ceremony.

You may not omit a preposition that is an indivisible part of a verb, even when leaving it in sounds awkward.

No: Two moves in a year is a lot to expect the children to adjust.

Yes: Two moves in a year is a lot to expect the children to adjust *to*.

No: He gave me the job, which I will be for the rest of my life grateful.

Yes: He gave me the job, *for* which I will be for the rest of my life grateful.

In such cases, you're probably better off rewriting.

The children may have trouble adjusting to moving twice in a year.

He gave me the job, for which I'll always be grateful.

In a Series, Be Consistent in Your Use of Prepositions

No: I asked her whether she planned to travel with him *to* India, China, and *to* Korea.

Yes: I asked her whether she planned to travel with him *to* India, *to* China, and *to* Korea.

What's the Problem?

Loading up your sentence with prepositions, although it isn't incorrect, makes for boring, hard-to-read prose. Don't let this happen to you!

The baby in the stroller by the entrance to the theater in the mall off the highway was crying.

You have two choices. You may, as in the "Yes" example, repeat the preposition before each item in the series. Or you may introduce a series with a preposition: *in* India, China, and Korea. The preposition then need not and should not be repeated. This is probably the way it's done most frequently:

> Jerry Karoff has advanced degrees *from* Princeton, Yale, and Harvard.

> I offered to help *in* any way, shape, or form I could.

Be Careful Not to Add Unnecessary Prepositions

No: She considers Paul *as* a great friend.

Yes: She considers Paul a great friend.

No: An indentured servant's term of service was typically *for* seven years.

Yes: An indentured servant's term of service was typically seven years.

With Your Prepositions, Stick to Standard Usage

The expression, for example, is *between (a) and (b)*, not *between (a) to (b)*:

No: The temperature varied *between* 20 degrees in the early morning *to* around 65 degrees by midafternoon.

Yes: The temperature varied between 20 degrees in the early morning *and* around 65 degrees by midafternoon.

Observe the Rules for a Couple of Important Preposition Pairs

among and *between*

The Usage Panel of the *American Heritage Dictionary* gives 28 lines to demystifying this distinction, so you know it's not simple and straightforward. There is a sort of rule that *between* is used when referring to two, *among* when referring to three or more of anything.

> The tiny cake was shared *among* the three hungry men.

> Caleb hunkered down in the little space *between* the living room and the hall.

Though this sounds easy enough, in fact, the difference between the two words can get complicated. Sometimes when you use the rule, it comes out sounding funny. What do you do, for example, about the treaty signed in 1945 *between* England, France, and Russia? "*Among* England, the United States, and Russia" sounds awful, and it is. So there's a useful addition to the rule, which says that if activity is going on between each pair—England and the United States, England and Russia, Russia and the United States—then *between* should be used. I tend to do it by ear, and I haven't gotten caught yet. If the distinction seems unclear, and if the whole thing makes you uncomfortable, simply rewrite: "The treaty was signed by England, the United States, and Russia."

in and *into*

If you are *in* a place, the word denotes your position. *Into*, by contrast, implies motion toward the inside:

> If I am *in* the tub, the phone is sure to ring.

> I got *into* the tub as soon as I was finished shoveling.

on and *onto*

Same as *in* and *into*: *On* implies being there; *onto* implies moving toward being there.

> Her wallet was where she had left it, *on* the table in the restaurant.

> Matt climbed *onto* the bureau before I could stop him.

Guard Against "Preposition Overload"

Not really a grammatical fault, this error can nonetheless spoil your prose. You may be writing loosely because you're feeling lazy. Or you may be working in an information-heavy environment that can tempt you to add fact after fact to your sentence. In either case, the result can be a slew of prepositional phrases difficult for a reader to wade through.

> The objection of the lawyer for the defense to the testimony of the witness to the slaying in Greenway Park was overruled.

Try weeding out a few of the prepositional phrases by telescoping your constructions:

> The defense lawyer's objection to the witness's testimony about the Greenway Park slaying was overruled.

Know Which Preposition to Use

As the following examples show, English is anything but consistent in the use of prepositions:

bored *with* my life	BUT	tired *of* waiting for you
forbid you *to* see him	BUT	prohibit passengers *from* standing
eager *to* get away	BUT	desirous *of* discovering her secret
collided *with* a car	BUT	crashed *into* a tree
devoid *of* feeling	BUT	lacking *in* human kindness
disappointed *in* you	BUT	afraid *for* you
with respect to	BUT	*in* regard to

If you're not sure whether it should be *in* or *by*, *Words into Type* has compiled a list of literally hundreds of nouns and verbs and the prepositions that go with them—16 pages last time I checked.

✹ IN BRIEF

> Place a prepositional phrase as close as possible to what it's describing.

> Be aware of placing a preposition at the end of a sentence.

> Omit prepositions if your meaning remains clear.

> In a series, be consistent in your use of prepositions.

> Be careful not to add unnecessary prepositions.

> With your prepositions, stick to standard usage.

> Observe the rules for a couple of important preposition pairs.

> Guard against "preposition overload."

> Know which preposition to use.

MAKE SURE YOU'VE GOT IT!

Are the following uses of prepositions correct, incorrect, or just unlovely?

1. I went to Barbara's because I needed a shoulder to cry on.

2. Don't save any of that manicotti for Steve and I.
3. He risked to climb into the chasm because Anne's life hung in the balance.
4. Belinda is considered to be a very attractive woman.
5. I brought equipment for the climb, the tent, and for cooking.
6. The last of the rations was shared among the soldiers on Christmas Day.
7. I wonder to what miracle the improvement in John's manners is due to.
8. The monkey with the bunch of bananas in the cage at the zoo in San Diego charmed us.
9. Bored of endless hours of piecework on the erg, I went in the boathouse and yelled for Ernest.
10. Was there another proto-human between Neanderthal man and Homo sapiens?
11. Fergus the cat was comfortably curled up on Harry's bed.
12. To Susan and he, zoning to control McMansion building is all-important.
13. Viewers have paid little attention to our revamped news hour and have taken no notice at all to the new sitcom *Mad at You*.

Answer Key

1. CORRECT: I went to Barbara's because I needed a shoulder to cry on.
2. INCORRECT: Don't save any of that manicotti for Steve and *me.*
3. INCORRECT: He risked *climbing* into the chasm because Anne's life hung in the balance.
4. UNLOVELY: Belinda is considered *a* very attractive woman.
5. INCORRECT: I brought equipment for the climb, *for* the tent, and for cooking.
6. CORRECT: The last of the rations was shared among the soldiers on Christmas Day.

7. INCORRECT: I wonder to what miracle the improvement in John's manners is *due*.

8. CORRECT BUT UNLOVELY: The *caged* monkey with the bunch of bananas *at the San Diego Zoo* charmed us.

9. INCORRECT: Bored *with* endless hours of piecework on the erg, I went *into* the boathouse and yelled for Ernest.

10. CORRECT: Was there another proto-human between Neanderthal man and Homo sapiens?

11. CORRECT: Fergus the cat was comfortably curled up on Harry's bed.

12. INCORRECT: To Susan and *him,* zoning to control McMansion building is all-important.

13. INCORRECT: Viewers have paid little attention to our revamped news hour and have taken no notice at all *of* the new sitcom *Mad at You.*

PART II
WRITE IT RIGHT!

Now that you've pinned the parts of speech into their proper corners, let's look at some elements of writing that, when done properly, make you look assured and in control of your material. The following chapters deal with the interface, or interacting, of the parts of speech to good or evil effect. (Hint: You want to be on the good side.)

This section, as G.K. Chesterson said of pond water closely examined, fairly teems with quiet fun. These issues are fun to talk and write about. You'll see examples of things people write incorrectly, sometimes to no laughable effect. Just remember that you don't want to be one of the folks being laughed at: This is not that kind of laughter that wins over people of importance. They laugh, and then they throw your application into the circular file. So enjoy, but pay close attention.

7

Agreement: Maintaining Good Relationships

Agreement is a major player in wrestling grammar to the ground. Read on.

In this chapter we investigate one of the easiest ways to be correct and appeal to readers of all kinds—by making sure all the components of a sentence agree.

To put it most simply, subjects and verbs must agree with one another. Pronouns must agree with subjects and objects.

For example, a singular subject—let's call her Jane—takes a verb that is singular as well. First, we say *Jane is* and *Jane arrives*, not *Jane are* and *Jane arrive*, which are plural verbs that need plural subjects (*Jane and Don are, job offers arrive*). Not very hard so far. Second, pronouns—those words that stand for one or more persons, such as *I, you, him, us*, and *their*—must agree with whomever they are standing in for. We say if referring to one male person, *he is*, and if referring to a group, she told *them*.

So why am I dedicating a chapter to agreement, which sounds incredibly easy? You'd never say, and certainly wouldn't write, *Jane are* or she told *him* if you meant several *hims*.

Well, because English comes in many shades of gray. Many, many shades—taupe may well be involved. Sometimes, for instance, it's not easy to tell whether a subject is singular or plural. Sometimes your verbs play tricks on you. And sometimes what you've learned may not be correct. (Does this make you feel paranoid? Good. I'm doing my job.) For example, should you write *number is* or *number are? Seven hours seem* or *Seven hours seems?*

Here are the issues of agreement that seem to bamboozle the most people the most frequently.

Collective Nouns Include Numbers of Persons or Things

Staff in the sense of people working is a collective noun; *group* is another. A collective or group noun takes a singular or plural verb depending on whether action is taken individually or as a unit. If the verb describes action that's taken by all, use a singular verb:

> The team *has decided* to hire a psychologist who specializes in love addiction interventions.

> The staff vehemently *opposes* working on New Year's Day.

If the action is taken individually, on the other hand, the verb should be plural.

> For Parents' Day, the class *are dressing* in their parents' old clothes.

> The prison population *were writing* revolutionary slogans on the walls of their cells.

It's comforting to note that in the latter case, you **must** either choose the plural verbs or write nonsense: *the class is dressing in its parents' old clothes? The population was writing revolutionary slogans on the walls of its cell?*

Certain Collective Nouns—*All, Almost, Fraction, Majority, More, Most,* and *Percentage*—Have Special Rules

To no one's great surprise, here come some exceptions. I may have missed some of these nouns and pronouns of quantity: The *American Heritage Dictionary of the English Language* is surprisingly helpful, among others. These collective nouns take a singular or plural verb depending on whether what's being collected is singular or plural:

> A large percentage of the *voters are dissatisfied* with our senator.

> A large percentage of the *state favors* the death penalty.

> More of my *friends are* vegetarians than strict vegans.

> Most of the *roast beef was eaten* immediately.

Note that these are exceptions! Don't begin thinking every word followed by *of* will behave this way. In the overwhelming majority of cases, the subject of the sentence, not the object of a prepositional phrase, governs the number of the verb.

> The <u>location</u> (subject) of the <u>cows</u> (object of prepositional phrase) *is* (not *are*) not my problem.

> The <u>theme</u> (subject) of those <u>movies</u> (object of prepositional phrase) *gives* (not *give*) me the shivers.

Number (the Word) Has Two Surprising Rules

Another exception, and this one is frankly amazing. If you say "*the* number" of whatever, the verb is singular. If you say "*a* number," the verb is plural.

> *The* number of people voting for Bush *was* astonishing.

> *A* number of us *have volunteered* to get off the bus.

How on earth do you suppose that happened? Again, we're dealing with an exception. If English is your native language, now might be a good time to offer up a prayer of thanksgiving. You probably do a lot of this by ear.

Some Nouns Are Plural, but Look Singular

They are in fact Latin plurals, and they have a singular form, ending in *um*, that's rarely used:

Data

No: *Is* the data on twins separated at birth ready for tonight's telecast?

Yes: *Are* the data on twins separated at birth ready for tonight's telecast?

Bacteria

No: The bacteria that *causes* necrotizing fasciitis *is* highly aggressive.

Yes: The bacteria that *cause* necrotizing fasciitis *are* highly aggressive.

> **Try It!**
>
> Only a fraction of the material on the Internet *is/are* of interest to me.
>
> Only a fraction of the students *say/says* they'd rather die than be home schooled.
>
> Answer: is, say

Media

No: The media *is predicting* a huge win for the senator from Alaska.

Yes: The media *are predicting* a huge win for the senator from Alaska.

Phenomenon/phenomena (Greek word) and *stratum/strata* belong to this same family, though their singular forms are more familiar. Actually, we do use *medium*, the singular form of *media*, regularly as well, but with a somewhat different meaning:

> You can capture an outdoor scene quickly through the medium of watercolors.

You'll often hear *the data is*. The usage may be changing. As with many constructions, if you aren't comfortable with writing *the data are* you can always rewrite the sentence:

> Do you have the data on twins ready for tonight's telecast?

Sometimes Plural Nouns Take Singular Verbs

Isn't English a riot? At the beginning of the chapter I mentioned *Seven hours seem* versus *Seven hours seems*. Again, I'm willing to bet your ear guides you in choosing correctly, but in writing people get tense, which they should—writing is documentation, after all. Your mistakes just sit there and glare at you. The rule is that when you are writing about a chunk of something, rather than its individual pieces, you generally use a singular verb. Take a look:

> *Seven hours seems* like a long time to wait for tickets.

> *Twenty-two clowns is* more than the Volkswagen will hold.

> *One hundred dollars has* been added to your account.

That last one comes with a special thumbing of the nose to a now-defunct bank whose automated banking system used to tell me, "One hundred dollars *have* been added." Doesn't it look funny? It sounded even worse. That's because it's the total amount of dollars, not the individual dollar bills, that is the focus of the sentence.

Some Words Always Take Singular Verbs

| anybody, anyone | each | somebody, someone | neither |
| nobody, no one | every | everybody, everyone | either |

Each of us *wants* to give you something special as a wedding present.

Neither girl *was* eager to set foot in the bat cave.

Either of the guides routinely *drives* these large buses.

Or and *Nor* Do Not Create Plural Subjects

Saul or Harvey gets my vote for too sexy for his shirt.

The Honda Prius or the Saturn AURA Green Line is my choice for my next car.

But what if you have both a singular and a plural subject?

John Carter or his brothers *has/have* my gun?

The rule is that you use a singular or plural verb depending on whether the subject **nearest the verb** is singular or plural. Therefore in the case of the Carter brothers, it's *have* my gun.

I or my colleagues at Masque and Mime *are judging* the contest for best costume.

Neither the girls nor their chaperone *is* coming tonight.

If that second sentence sounds awkward to you, just reorder the subjects or rewrite:

Reordered: Neither the chaperone nor the girls *are coming* tonight.

Rewritten: The girls and their chaperone *won't be coming* tonight.

As Well As, In Addition To, With, and *Including* Do Not Create Plural Subjects Either

As we speak, Biffie the dog, with his trainer, the owner, and some groupies, *is entering* the ring at the Westminster Kennel Club Dog Show.

Wellesley College, in addition to the rest of the former Seven Sisters colleges, *is offering* a very generous financial aid package.

Everyone in the household, including the cats, *is coming* to watch Marla graduate from nursing school.

"One of Those Things" Is a Special Case

An argument grammarians regularly have with editors, friends, and family concerns a sentence such as "She's one of those diehards who prefer ocean to pool swimming." This is correct. People complain that *of those diehards* is a prepositional phrase that can be lifted right out of the sentence, leaving "She's one who prefers ocean swimming," which is of course grammatically correct: The subject *she* agrees with the single verb *prefers*. Unfortunately, this isn't the way the construction works.

Why doesn't it work that way? Because "who prefer ocean to pool swimming" refers to the diehards, not to the lady: it's "diehards who prefer," not "one who prefers." Turn it around and you can see how it works: "Of those people who prefer ocean to pool swimming, she is one."

The *Boston Globe* quoted an elite Boston Marathon runner on a dismal showing:

> "It's just one of those things that *happen*." (italics mine)

The following are all correctly written:

> It's one of those awful days that *make* you wish you hadn't gotten up.

> Do you think he's one of those dreadful composers who *don't* bother with rhythm?

> Peter is one of those unfortunates who *faint* whenever they *donate* blood.

As for the people who think you can simply chop out "of those things" from the first sentence, proving it's "one...that *makes*," the trick just plain doesn't work: "It's one that makes you wish you hadn't gotten up." One what? You really can't leave the phrase out; the sentence doesn't make sense without it. That is your clue that the phrase is crucial to the sentence and that the rest of the sentence sticks like glue to it; in fact, the phrase runs for the rest of the sentence—the whole phrase is *of those awful days that make you wish you hadn't gotten up*. Try another: Take the last sentence and make the verb agree with *Peter*. It reads, "Peter is one of those unfortunates who faints whenever he donates blood." I don't know about you, but I'm reacting poorly to "unfortunates who faints."

One of those (whatevers) has a friendly, informal sound and may be appropriate for the writing you do. If you want to use it, remember that the verb does not agree with the subject, but with the object of the prepositional phrase. If this bothers you, it's no trouble to rewrite without it:

Like many people, she prefers ocean to pool swimming.

Is he among those dreadful composers who don't bother with rhythm?

Make Sure Pronouns Are in the Correct Case

I've given a full chapter to pronouns on their own, so this is just a mention here of the grammar glitches they can help propel you into. Pronouns stand in, or substitute, for a subject or object.

Jesse went to the mall.

She went to the mall.

I love Jesse.

I love *her*.

As you can see from these examples, pronouns change case depending on their use in a sentence. They are the only nouns in English that retain special endings—reminding us of the German and Latin origins of English. We call this phenomenon **case**. If Jesse is the subject, the noun performing the action, the pronoun is in the subject case:

Jesse went.

She went.

If Jesse is the object, the noun being done to, the pronoun will be in the object case:

I love *her*.

Here are the most important subject and object pronouns.

	Subject Case	Object Case
Singular	I	me
	you	you
	he, she, it	him, her, it
	who	whom
Plural	we	us
	you	you
	they	them
	who	whom

You would never write, or even think, "Her went to the mall," nor would you write "I love she." Yet every day people as smart as you are writing the equivalent. Look:

> *Her and John* got married in a Las Vegas chapel.

> The usher told *him and I* there were no more seats available.

If you look separately at the two halves of the subject *Her and John*, you'll realize how horribly incorrect the sentence is as written. *Her* got married? I don't think so. Same with the object *he and I*: The usher told *him* is fine, but the usher told *I*?

The fix is very simple: Just use each part of the subject separately in your sentence. If it sounds awful, you've got the wrong pronoun case.

You can also create pronoun disagreement by referring to a singular subject or object with a plural pronoun.

> The *business manager* is an integral part of the team, and *they are* sometimes *ignored* by the Head of School.

> First, ask the *passenger* whether *they have* liquids or a knife.

Do you see that the business manager is being called *they*? Likewise the passenger? As for "the business manager are ignored" and "the passenger have," that's not English.

These errors may represent an effort to be gender-neutral: The writer didn't want to write *he* or *him* and be called sexist. (Or write *she* and offend all men.) But please note that good intentions do not a correct sentence make. Furthermore, you can almost always find a way to write around them. For example:

> The business manager, an integral part of the team, is sometimes ignored by the Head of School.

OR

> Business managers, integral to the team, are sometimes ignored by the Head of School.

Whenever Possible, Keep Your Subject and Verb Close Together

Agreement problems are much easier to flag and correct if you don't have a lot of words crowded in between the subject of your sentence and its verb. This sounds easier than it is. We are all trying to cram so much information into our writing that it's tempting to add a fact here, a fact there, and it's harder to hold onto that subject-verb connection. You can wind up with an unsightly grammar predicament.

> The *sum* of all of Rachel's coins, both foreign and American, old and new, which she'd collected since she was 12, *were* worth about $5,000.

The subject of this sentence is *sum*. The verb is *were*. The only problem is, you can't say *the sum were*, right? What's happened is that our writer became fascinated with the various characteristics of the coin collection and, concentrating on these, believed the subject was *coins*—understandably, because so much material got stuffed in between subject and verb.

You can even prompt a misreading by allowing too great a distance between the two.

> Let *tulips* from Holland and all the rest of the lovely profusion of early flowers of the spring *dance* in your garden.

Well, as a casual reader you could be forgiven for thinking someone was holding a spring dance in the garden. The flower farm ad copy needs an editing.

Don't let this happen to you! Take a look, after you've written, and make sure your subject (whatever's doing the action) and your verb (whatever's being done) aren't widely separated.

✸ IN BRIEF

- ⟩ Collective nouns include numbers of persons or things.
- ⟩ Certain collective nouns—*all, almost, fraction, majority, more, most,* and *percentage*—have special rules.
- ⟩ Number (the word) has two surprising rules.
- ⟩ Some nouns are plural, but look singular.
- ⟩ Sometimes plural nouns take singular verbs.
- ⟩ Some words always take singular verbs.
- ⟩ *Or* and *nor* do not create plural subjects.

> *As well as*, *in addition to*, *with*, and *including* do not create plural subjects either.
> *"One of those things"* is a special case.
> Make sure pronouns are in the correct case.
> Whenever possible, keep your subject and verb close together.

MAKE SURE YOU'VE GOT IT!

Find and correct errors of agreement in the following sentences if necessary.

1. My staff is bringing their own lunches to the company picnic.
2. A large portion of our retirement savings are earmarked for long-term care.
3. Everyone in my book club and yours say *The Dante Club* is awful.
4. The cousins or Jamie think they can come to the reunion.
5. A majority of the campers dislikes getting up at dawn.
6. Sebastien met she and Margaret and utterly charmed them.
7. Each of us are trying to understand the other's point of view.
8. What percentage of the voting bloc are Hispanic?
9. Ursula, with her three vice presidents, have dibs on the conference room.
10. When a person turns 16, they may apply for a license in Pennsylvania.
11. Two hundred dollars are way too much to pay for running shoes.
12. The group has collected money for a present for our tour guide.
13. I am one of those skiers who heads for the lodge when it's 32 degrees or below.
14. Neither of us want to go on the Matterhorn ride.
15. The bacteria moves with frightening speed into the lungs.

16. Her and I have missed Aunt Veronica a lot since she disappeared.

Answer Key

1. My staff *are* bringing their own lunches to the company picnic.

2. A large portion of our retirement savings *is* earmarked for long-term care.

3. Everyone in my book club and yours *says* *The Dante Club* is awful.

4. *Jamie or the cousins* think they can come to the reunion.

5. A majority of the campers *dislike* getting up at dawn.

6. Sebastien met *her* and Margaret and utterly charmed them.

7. Each of us *is* trying to understand the other's point of view.

8. What percentage of the voting bloc *is* Hispanic?

9. Ursula, with her three vice presidents, *has* dibs on the conference room.

10. When *you turn* 16, *you* may apply for a license in Pennsylvania.

11. Two hundred dollars *is* way too much to pay for running shoes.

12. The group has collected money for a present for our tour guide. CORRECT AS WRITTEN

13. I am one of those skiers who *head* for the lodge when it's 32 degrees or below.

14. Neither of us *wants* to go on the Matterhorn ride.

15. The bacteria *move* with frightening speed into the lungs.

16. *She* and I have missed Aunt Veronica a lot since she disappeared.

Possessives: Where Does the Darned Apostrophe Go?

Many print cartridges have been exhausted over the correct way to create the possessive form of various nouns, whether the apostrophe goes before or after an *s*, whether the s was already there or had to be added, and so forth. It's pretty simple as long as you know what kind of noun you've got.

To Form the Possessive of a Single Noun, Add *'s*

John	*John's* pen
the world	the *world's* greatest dad
Mr. Wilbur	Mr. *Wilbur's* house
the YMCA	the *YMCA's* rules

By the way, you may have heard the rule that possessives apply only to people. The rule is old and often disobeyed. Note "the *world's* greatest dad"—but be aware that some people still regard it as standard.

To Form the Possessive of a Single Noun *Ending in s,* Also Add *'s*

bus	the *bus's* brakes
Charles	*Charles's* shoes
waitress	the *waitress's* attitude
Mrs. Van Ness	Mrs. Van *Ness's* husband

There was an era in which teachers told their students that if the single noun ended in *s* you could simply add an apostrophe. That was a while ago, and I hope you didn't learn it. Every good authority I know—let's start with the bible of them all, the *Chicago*

Manual of Style—insists that you use 's. If you learned the incorrect form, I'm sorry. Let's curse Mrs. Frumpbottomly from fourth grade and get on with it.

There is in fact good reason to use the full 's even on words that end in *s*. Try saying, for example, *Charles's shoes*. You actually pronounce the 's, which makes it abundantly clear you are saying "the shoes belonging to Charles"—as opposed, say, to a brand of shoes: "Charles Shoes." Or "Charl's Shoes." Horrors.

There are a few exceptions, mostly ancient names. Some biblical names, for example, drop the second *s*, as do some Greek names.

> I taught Business Writing to adults for quite a few years and always had a hard time convincing my classes that a name ending in *s* forms the possessive by adding 's. In one class I was blessed with a student named Alexis. When she raised her hand during the class on 's, I expected resistance, but Alexis informed us that her teacher in an early grade had insisted that it was *Alexis's desk,* not *Alexis' desk.* Quite a mouthful for a little kid: My class was powerfully impressed.

Jesus	*Jesus'* teachings
Moses	*Moses'* rod
Socrates	*Socrates'* followers
Mr. Paleologos	Mr. *Paleologos'* 2008 tax return

And there are a few phrases with *sake* in which by custom the *s* is dropped:

for *appearance'* sake   for *goodness'* sake   for *conscience'* sake

I recommend an exception also for the possessive form of *the United States*. We refer to this country nowadays in the singular: "The United States *is* committed to providing aid to Africa." So it should be "the United States's commitment." Yet, perhaps because of the fact that *states* is in fact a plural word, "the United States' commitment" feels correct. If you aren't comfortable with that—or for that matter with any possessive form—you can simply rewrite.

the commitment of the United States

the brakes of the bus

the shoes Charles is wearing

the biotech firms of Massachusetts (*Massachusetts's* is truly unwieldy.)

Now it gets easier.

To Form the Possessive of a Plural Noun Ending in *s*, Add an Apostrophe

the stores	the *stores'* hours
the Rockies	the *Rockies'* grandeur
the businesses	the *businesses'* locations
the ladies	the *ladies'* choice
the Davidsons	the *Davidsons'* oldest son
the Harrises	the *Harrises'* party

Look at that last entry: the Harrises and their party. People have trouble, not just with the possessive, but with the simple plural, of names ending in *s*, so let's break here to clear up any confusion. For a family name, you add *s* or *es* to the name when speaking of the whole family. Accordingly, the possessive, following our rule, is simply an apostrophe:

Mr. Dane	the Danes	the Danes' dog
Ms. Jones	the Joneses	the Joneses' house
Mrs. Inverness	the Invernesses	the Invernesses' maple tree
Mr. Andrews	the Andrewses	the Andrewses' invitation

Remember: If you are going to put your name on the mailbox, it's *The Joneses*. If you want to put a sign on the house to show it's your family's house, it's *The Joneses'*—not *The Jones's*, *The Jones'es*, or *The Jone's*. No kidding: I've seen it and it isn't pretty.

To Form the Possessive of a Plural Noun That Doesn't End in *s*, Add *'s*

men	the *men's* club
women	*women's* rights
people	*people's* feelings
mice	the *mice's* nests
attorneys general	the *attorneys general's* views

I think I'd write "the views of the attorneys general" on that last one, actually.

Pronouns NEVER Take Apostrophes

Pronouns, which are words that stand in for nouns, such as *me* and *they*, form possessives differently from the rest of the nouns. Here's a chart that shows the possessive pronouns:

Subject Pronoun	Possessive, Adjective Form	Possessive, Noun Form
I	my	mine
you	your	yours
he	his	his
she	her	hers
it	its	its
we	our	ours
you	your	yours
they	their	theirs
who	whose	whose

Do you notice anything unusual about the possessive forms in the right-hand column? Although most of them end in *s*, **there are no apostrophes.** Because our English pronouns are ancient history—they've been around since before the 12th century—they are irregular. Maybe the apostrophe hadn't been invented. At any rate, this means you must never, ever write *her's, our's, your's,* or *their's* (unless you are a linguistics expert writing about a pronoun as a word, which isn't going to happen for most of us). Or *it's*, if you're using the pronoun from either column. There will never be an occasion for you to write *it's*, unless you mean *it is* or *it has*.

Take it as one of grammar's commandments: Thou shalt not add apostrophes to the pronouns.

Learn the difference between *your* and *you're!* If you aren't clear, your writing will look inexpert and unfortunately your spell checker is badly mixed up as well, so *you're* on *your* own. (This little phrase is meant to be a memory aid.) Here's the full story:

Your is a pronoun, a possessive adjective from the second column of the chart on page 85.

You're is a contraction of *you are.* It's can be a homonym of *your,* depending on the way it's pronounced, but you can see that the meanings are entirely different.

Add a Possessive Only to the Last Name in a Series if Each Owns Something in Common; If Possession Is Not Joint, Make All Names Possessive

If two or more people possess something in common, you need only put your apostrophe or 's after the last name.

Larry, Moe, and Curly's show

Mary and Tobias's son

If, on the other hand, each possesses his or her own show, or son, or whatever, you must put an apostrophe after each.

General Washington's and General Braddock's troops

the applause for Terry's and Grace's speeches

✹ IN BRIEF

> To form the possessive of a single noun, add 's.

> To form the possessive of a single noun *ending in s,* also add 's.

> To form the possessive of a plural noun ending in *s,* add an apostrophe.

> To form the possessive of a plural noun that doesn't end in *s,* add 's.

> Pronouns NEVER take apostrophes.

⧁ Add a possessive only to the last name in a series if each owns something in common; if possession is not joint, make all names possessive.

MAKE SURE YOU'VE GOT IT!

Try your hand at substituting possessive forms for the italicized phrases. Example:

Give me *the time card of you.* = Give me *your* time card.

1. In spite of what he says, I did not spill wine on *the shirt of the man.*
2. Be sure to get a good look at *the new digital camera of her.*
3. Don't let Lenore take *the boots of the children* off in the living room.
4. Maybe next year you'll be invited to *the barbecue of Mr. and Mrs. Jones.*
5. I was astonished that *the wolfhound of Boris* was so large.
6. I was thrilled to meet *the brother of Althea and Rodney.*
7. *The teachings of Jesus and Buddha* remain a cornerstone of ethics as it is taught today.
8. *The main interest of the men* seems to be golf.
9. The first apartment on the second floor is *the one belonging to them.*
10. Don't ask to see *the pictures of Tex* unless you want to be there all night.
11. We're already six months late filing *the tax forms of the business.*
12. It is clear that the independent candidate is *the choice of the people.*
13. At the museum exhibit, Fashion Since Eve, I was fascinated by *the shoes of the ladies.*
14. BONUS QUESTION: Which form, *your* or *you're*, is correct in the following sentence?

    You're/Your lucky I didn't put a bullet hole in *you're/your* nice white tuxedo shirt!

Answer Key

1. In spite of what he says, I did not spill wine on *the man's shirt*.
2. Be sure to get a good look at *her new digital camera*.
3. Don't let Lenore take *the children's boots* off in the living room.
4. Maybe next year you'll be invited to *Mr. and Mrs. Jones's barbecue*.
5. I was astonished that *Boris's wolfhound* was so large.
6. I was thrilled to meet *Althea and Rodney's brother*.
7. *Jesus' and Buddha's teachings* remain a cornerstone of ethics as it is taught today.
8. *The men's main interest* seems to be golf.
9. The first apartment on the second floor is *theirs*.
10. Don't ask to see *Tex's pictures* unless you want to be there all night.
11. We're already six months late filing *the business's tax forms*.
12. It is clear that the independent candidate is *the people's choice*.
13. At the museum exhibit, Fashion Since Eve, I was fascinated by *the ladies' shoes*.
14. BONUS QUESTION:

    You're lucky I didn't put a bullet hole in *your* nice white tuxedo shirt.

Parallel Construction: Not a Hard-Hat Job

A good example of parallel construction is *Lord of the Rings: The Two Towers*. I'm kidding. Parallel construction is a writing technique that helps make your work look both attractive and professional. Best of all, unlike building construction, it's easy and you don't need a helmet.

Parallelism is about items that are alike. Parallel lines in geometry run in the same direction. Parallel ideas—yours and mine—are similar: Our minds are running on the same track. And parallelism in writing requires that parts of a sentence used in the same way be expressed in the same way. You may not have had any experience with this rule, which is too bad. Observing it will help shine up your writing style and put you in the paper pile of winners.

What do we mean when we say that parts used in the same way should be expressed in the same way? Take the observation that "it's usually better to kick on the fourth down than to run the ball." Reduced to its basics, the sentence says, "It's better *to this* than *to that*." As it's written, those two parts balance; they match, because both are expressed as *to* verbs: *to kick, to run*. But if the sentence was to read, "It's better to kick on the fourth down than running the ball," though it would still be more or less grammatical, it would be clumsy and—what's the word I

> ### What's the Problem?
> When you don't use parallel construction, your writing:
> - May confuse your reader.
> - Will be less attractive.
> - May contain grammatical errors.

want? Not a nice word. Gross, maybe. Loserly. Dorky, which my *Webster's* defines as "foolishly inept." You don't want to be guilty of foolishly inept prose.

Use Parallel Structure to Make Your Writing Clear

Suppose you're the secretary of the dance committee, taking minutes as the committee begins plans for the Spring Fling. Here's how you might record a preliminary list of what needs to be dealt with:

> The committee needs to
>> Develop a budget
>> Choose a location
>> Subcommittees: food, band, decorations, transportation
>> Investigating ways to raise money
>> To plan publicity

Notice I said "preliminary." If this list is going to circulate beyond your notebook, it needs work. Why? Try reading each of those items with the introductory phrase. "The committee needs to develop a budget, the committee needs to choose a location, the committee needs to subcommittees: food," "the committee needs to investigating ways." Hold it. That's not English, and "the committee needs to to plan publicity" isn't either. That's because the five items on your agenda are not in parallel form.

Fixing this is pretty easy. You're probably there already. Simply change the parts of speech *so the lead-in (the first part of the sentence) makes sense with every one of the following items*. If I decide to leave the first two, which read sensibly enough, then I need to make verbs out of the following three. Now my vertical list reads this way:

> The committee needs to
>> Develop a budget
>> Choose a location
>> Form subcommittees: food, band, transportation
>> Investigate ways to raise money
>> Plan publicity

You could also rework the introduction to make sense with five noun constructions:

The committee needs the following:

Budget

Location

Subcommittees: food, band, transportation

Money-raising ideas

Publicity campaign

So within your series, you should stick with items that are similar in form. Take, for example, this sentence from *The Hungry Ocean* by Linda Greenlaw:

Carl and Kenny were both busy cutting hooks from sharks' mouths, clearing what was left of the leaders, and throwing the sharks back overboard.

Cutting, clearing, and *throwing.* Verbs of a feather flock together. It's easy to understand where we're heading with this matched series of *–ing* verb forms, and it's pleasant to read.

On the other hand, it's equally *un*pleasant to get a sudden change of direction when reading—it feels as if the writer has jumped the rails and chugged off into the cornfield, which can give readers a nasty jolt. And a jolt can make them resentful, and then they begin to question the writer's content—not just how it's being said, but *what's* being said, and for you as the writer that's dangerous. Suppose, for example, Ms. Greenlaw had written her sentence this way:

Clark and Kenny were both busy cutting hooks from sharks' mouths, clearing what was left of the leaders, and then they threw the sharks back overboard.

See how the rhythm is disrupted?

Use Parallel Structure to Make Your Writing More Attractive

Parallel construction is a device writers and especially speechmakers often use to make their words flow gracefully, eloquently, and memorably. (Note the series of –*ly* words. These are parallel adverbs, adverbs being words telling *how* something is done.) Good authors have done this for ages. Abraham Lincoln's Gettysburg Address is not a long piece, but it contains at least 17 examples of parallel construction, depending on how you count. That's one reason it's so memorable today. Well, *yesterday* students actually used to memorize the Gettysburg Address and recite it at assemblies. Parallelism such as "The world will little note nor long remember what we say here, but it can never forget what they did here" made it easier to remember, which is a good definition of memorable in my book. Lincoln's use of parallel construction also helps get a rhythm going that's pleasing to read:

> ...and that government of the people, by the people, and for the people shall not perish from the earth.

Often parallelism is combined with word repetition that impresses itself on the mind. Lincoln does this as well in the previous example. So did General Colin Powell, giving a speech in Boston in which he described Colonel Robert Gould Shaw and his 54th Regiment, marching

> ...on their way to hope, on their way to glory, and for many of them, on their way to death.

No need to abuse the obvious. The point is that the more easily your reader understands, the more readily you'll communicate and the more that very important person will like your work.

Use Parallel Structure to Help Ensure That Your Writing Is Correct

The committee agenda from earlier in the chapter and the following lines illustrate something you especially don't want in your writing: the dreaded *false series*.

> Thanks a lot, Cyndi. When you returned my personal mix CD, it was scratched, loaded with skips, and the box was missing.

A false series is usually ugly because its construction isn't parallel, and often it's wrong because it's a grammatical error as well. Cue up Cyndi again and break out the last part.

> When you sent back my personal mix CD, it was
>> scratched
>> loaded with skips, and
>> the box was missing.

The lead-in *it was* functions in the exact same way the lead-in of agenda items for the dance committee (*The committee needs*). Again, when a series goes vertical, the mistake glares at you. One of these things is not like the others; one of these things doesn't belong! "It was the box was missing" is gibberish. The diagram form makes it clear that all three items in the series must read logically with *it was*, and the last should match the form of the adjectives (descriptive words) *scratched* and *loaded with skips*. Here's one way to accomplish this:

> When you sent back my personal mix CD, it was
>> scratched,
>> loaded with skips, and
>> boxless

Or *missing its box*. Or anything that makes sense when read with *it was*.

Here's another black-hat example:

> The children presented a diverse holiday program, singing Christmas carols, a spirited rendition of the Chanukah song "Maoz Tzur," and performed a play based on the Kwanzaa story of the seven black swans.

Look what happens when we diagram this loser vertically:

> The children presented a diverse holiday program, singing
>> Christmas carols,
>> a spirited rendition of the Chanukah song "Maoz Tzur," and
>> performed a play based on the Kwanzaa story of the seven black swans.

"Singing performed a play"? Here's a fix, changing the introductory phrase:

> The children presented a diverse holiday program,
>> **singing** Christmas carols
>> **offering** a spirited rendition of the Chanukah song, and
>> **performing** a play based on the Kwanzaa story of the seven black swans.

Here's another, with internal parallels in bold type! See how much fun we're having?

> NOTE: After you diagram and fix your work, put it back into running sentence form.

> The children presented a diverse holiday program,
>
> > **singing** Christmas carols and a spirited rendition of the Chanukah song "Maoz Tzur" and
> >
> > **performing** a play based on the Kwanzaa story of the seven black swans.

Yet another, simply breaking the sentence into two:

> The schoolchildren presented a diverse holiday program, singing Christmas carols and a spirited rendition of the Chanukah song "Maoz Tzur." They also performed a play based on the Kwanzaa story of the seven black swans.

The underlying reason for parallel construction is that it helps the reader—professor, mentor, language-loving friend or relative—grasp your meaning easily. If you begin a series with a verb such as *singing*, the brain is "primed" to accept more verbs: offering, performing, whatever-ing. Or so the experts tell us, and it makes sense. So keep a close eye on your writing when you introduce a series of items, and be sure they are in parallel form.

✸ IN BRIEF

> Use parallel structure to make your writing clear.

> Use parallel structure to make your writing more attractive.

> Use parallel structure to help ensure that your writing is correct.

MAKE SURE YOU'VE GOT IT!

Correct nonparallel construction in the following examples:

1. Tell Edith I said to forget about the money and that she should get on with her life.

2. The Salem witches were hanged in 1623 instead of burning.

3. My company, Wyziwidget, is installing a gym, a comprehensive library, and a new cafeteria is planned.

4. I'm going to need intensive therapy, to rest several hours a day, and being visited often.

5. I liked Justin Timberlake when he was with 'N Sync better than his current solo albums.

6. Leonard is careful in business dealings, his family life, and in community work.

7. Sedona was a disappointment to the Jacksons, but Scottsdale was thrilling.

8. The lure of cash and being afraid of imprisonment led the robbers to turn on each other.

9. LuAnn is bright, competent, and has no scruples.

10. Dan Brown's thriller, *The Da Vinci Code*, is
    exciting
    contains a lot of interesting information
    it's not well written

11. The 14-year-old student was charged with three counts of malicious explosion, the crime of breaking and entering, and spent a night in the city jail.

12. The rose is my favorite flower, and my favorite bird is the cardinal.

Answer Key

There are many ways to correct these, and yours may be better than mine, but here are my suggestions.

1. Tell Edith I said to forget about the money ***and get on*** with her life.

2. The Salem witches were hanged in 1623, ***not burned***.

3. My company, Wyziwidget, is installing a gym ***and*** a comprehensive library, and a new cafeteria is planned.
   OR
   My company, Wyziwidget, is installing a gym, a comprehensive library, and ***a new cafeteria***.

4. I'm going to need intensive therapy, *several hours of rest each day, and frequent visitors*.

5. I liked *the albums* Justin Timberlake *made with* 'N Sync better than his current solo albums.

6. Leonard is careful in business dealings, *in* his family life, and in community work.

7. Sedona was *disappointing* to the Jacksons, but Scottsdale was thrilling.

8. The lure of cash and *the fear of imprisonment* led the robbers to turn on each other.

9. LuAnn is bright, competent, and *unscrupulous*.

10. Dan Brown's thriller, *The Da Vinci Code*, is
    exciting,
    *full of interesting information, and
    poorly written*.

11. The 14-year-old student was charged with three counts of malicious explosion *and* the crime of breaking and entering and spent a night in the city jail.

12. *My favorite flower is the rose*, and my favorite bird is the cardinal.

The Right Word:
Choose It and Use It

The words and phrases in this chapter are frequently abused, confused, and improperly used. If you feel a little shaky about any of them, mark them and refer to them before you write incorrectly and embarrass yourself. You can pick up a poor-writer label easily by writing *invoke* when you mean *evoke*. I've included some mnemonics, or memory aids, that I hope will be helpful. For more information, consult your dictionary, which can be surprisingly useful, especially when you're dealing with troublesome pairs. *The American Heritage Dictionary of the English Language, Fourth Edition,* is a good one. It even has a smart and illustrious Usage Panel that votes its approval or disapproval of disputed usage and includes the outcome. Fun with grammar!

abbreviation   a shortened version of a word or words

acronym   a word, often pronounceable, formed with the first letters (more or less) of words

NOTE: An acronym is a special kind of abbreviation, but not all abbreviations are acronyms.

Dr. is an *abbreviation* of the word *doctor*.

MADD is the *acronym* for the group Mothers Against Drunk Driving.

✳

adverse   bad or undesirable, usually applied to an inanimate object

averse   disinclined or reluctant, usually applied to a person

In an *adverse* reaction to criticism of his play, David screamed and cried.

I'm *averse* to discussing Charlie's college plans with a stranger.

✳

affect, v.　　to have an effect on; to cause emotion

effect, v.　　to cause or bring about

The humidity *affected* the paint, which didn't dry for weeks.

She *effected* an amazing change in their table manners.

It's easy to choose the right verb if you remember their functions in this sentence are in alphabetical order: I *affected* the plant by drying it out; I *effected* a solution by watering it.

Three other uses of *affect* and *effect* follow:

affect, v.　　to put on or fake

She *affects* the manners of a grande dame.

affect, n.　　a psychological term roughly corresponding to mood

He has a flat *affect*, showing no emotion over Sue's death.

effect, n.　　result

This cough medicine is not having the desired *effect*.

✳

afflict　　to cause suffering or pain to

inflict　　(on) to give (something unpleasant) (to)

These words are not interchangeable.

Familial arthritis *afflicted* him from the age of 40.

She was *afflicted* with a very bad temper.

John's reckless spending *inflicted* much pain on his mother.

Laura *inflicted* her ugly temper on everyone around her.

✳

ambiguous　　vague or unclear, able to be interpreted in different ways

ambivalent　　unable to decide, uncertain

Ambiguous is the way something appears; ambivalent is the way one feels about something.

The meaning of "do it in good time" is *ambiguous*.

I am *ambivalent* about staying with our friends for such a long time.

✳

as	similar to; precedes a verb
like	similar to; precedes a noun

I'm talking about why the odious expression "like I say" is incorrect. The rule is that *like* precedes a noun (or pronoun).

Like a bat out of hell, she ran for the exit.

The ship was steaming towards Naples *like a house afire*.

It'll help if you remember one of those clichés: *like a bat out of hell, like a house afire, like a queen, like a baby,* and *just like me,* are all proper uses of *like*. Remember the old song that begins "She looks like an angel"? A house, a queen, a baby, me, an angel—all nouns, all following *like*.

As, on the other hand, precedes a verb. In fact, it almost always precedes a complete sentence with a subject and verb:

The rate must be cut, *as the chairman observed*.

As I said (**never** like I said), Philip needs to grow up a little.

As expected, his proposal is late. (A verb in this case, but not a complete sentence. The verb must be there.)

You try it:

Arthur is acting _____ a complete jerk about plans for the weekend.

Why do you object to working nights _____ you've been doing all along?

Oscar has looked _____ a prince throughout the divorce proceedings.

It's *like, as, like,* and I'll bet you got all three. The noun and verb thing works every time.

While we're on the subject of *like,* I have two more rules.

1. Don't use *like* as a substitute for *as if* or *as though* in writing:

No: You look *like* you're lost.

Yes: You look *as if* you're lost.

No: The ship looks *like* it's aground.

Yes: The ship looks *as though* it's aground.

Although you'll probably get away with it in conversation, because conversation is written on air, *like* isn't strictly correct here, because the word is meant to suggest similarity, and *you* are not similar to *you're lost* any more than the ship is similar to *it's aground*. In writing, which can easily sit around and make you look bad, *as if* is the wiser choice.

2. Don't use it if you can substitute *such as*:

No: We need some strong guys, *like* Samson and Mr. Clean.

Yes: We need some strong guys, *such as* Samson and Mr. Clean.

No: I'd suggest some crime novels, *like* Sue Grafton's alphabet series.

Yes: I'd suggest some crime novels, *such as* Sue Grafton's alphabet series.

Again, the connecting word *like* implies a similarity; *such as* is more exact, implying that what follows is a part of what precedes it. That's probably why it sounds better than *like* in this case.

If you feel shaky on these distinctions, you can substitute *as*, *as if*, and *such as* for *like* to see whether any of the three works better:

She looks *like* her mother.

Try it. She looks *as* her mother? She looks *as if* her mother? She looks *such as* her mother? Not one sounds even remotely correct. *Like* is correct as written.

Let's try another:

The cuisine of hot countries *like* India and Mexico features many spicy foods.

> **A Never-Fail Method for Handling *Like***
>
> If you're not sure whether *like* is correct in your sentence, try substituting *as, as if,* and *such as.* If any of these sounds better, use it!

As India and Mexico? No complete sentence follows *as*, and it sounds bad. *As if* India and Mexico? Clearly wrong. *Such as* India and Mexico? Now we're getting somewhere. *Such as* is correct.

✳

can	am/is/are able to
may	have/has permission to

Of course you *can* drive the RV over Mrs. Jones's cockapoo. But you *may* not. Don't use *can* as a synonym for *may*.

No: The dean says Julie *can* come back two days late.

Yes: The dean says Julie *may* come back two days late.

No: *Can* I put my hand on your tummy to feel the baby kick?

Yes: *May* I put my hand on your tummy to feel the baby kick?

✳

compare to   to indicate that something or someone is
similar to another

compare with to put two things together and observe their
similarities and dissimilarities

She has been *compared to* Hillary Clinton.

Compared with last year's temperatures, this year's numbers show a
warming trend.

✳

complement   to add a useful dimension to; to help compose

compliment   to say something nice

That hat *complements* your outfit beautifully.

He *complimented* my outfit, saying it was quite becoming.

Ignore the advertising industry, which gets it wrong a lot of
the time.

✳

continual   repeated, over and over

continuous   steady, uninterrupted

We were distracted by *continual* interruptions from little Tom.

The *continuous* whine of the drill grates on the average patient.

Just remember the *a* in *continual* stands for "again and again";
the *ous* in *continuous* stands for "one uninterrupted sequence."

✳

council   governing organization

counsel, n.   advice; lawyer

counsel, v.   to advise

The *council* meets each Wednesday night.

His *counsel* has been enormously helpful.

Counsel is browbeating the witness.

I'd *counsel* you to ignore her insinuations.

It helps to remember that *council* has just the one meaning of a governing body; everything else is *counsel*.

✳

credible	believable
credulous	believing, gullible

Credible applies to a concept: an idea, a statement, a hypothesis. *Credulous* applies to a person or group of persons.

His theory about the "breathing" of tectonic plates seems *credible*.

The salesman wrapped his *credulous* audience around his little finger.

✳

discreet	prudent, showing self-restraint
discrete	separate, able to be counted

The wrong spelling has begun appearing in print more and more frequently. These words have entirely different meanings.

We can trust Harry: He's *discreet* and will keep our secret.

Hawaii is actually a chain of *discrete* islands.

✳

disinterested	unbiased, impartial
uninterested	bored, not interested

The meaning of these words has flip-flopped several times throughout several centuries, and some people use them interchangeably to mean not interested. I agree, however, with the dictionaries that stick with *disinterested* meaning impartial, like a good judge, and *uninterested* meaning lacking interest. It's a useful distinction.

You should have that hat appraised by a *disinterested* party.

Both girls appeared *uninterested* in touring the Museum of Thimbles.

✳

enormity	awful wickedness
enormousness	great size

Although badness is the primary meaning of *enormity*, most dictionaries will let you use it to mean great size also, especially if the dimensions inspire dread; be aware it has the separate sense of monstrous evil.

Jasper was appalled by the *enormity* of her violent act.

The *enormousness* of the theater so overwhelmed her that she forgot her lines.

✳

ensure   to make sure something happens; to guarantee

insure   to sell or buy insurance

Remember that *insure* refers to *ins*urance.

We have taken all possible precautions to *ensure* your safety.

Fortunately, Selma's wig was fully *insured* against fire.

✳

evoke   to draw forth or produce

invoke   to call on; to appeal to

Bill's tirade against women in sports *evoked* a surprisingly strong response from the boys.

Helen *invoked* the ghosts of Lee and Grant to aid in the reenactment of the surrender at Appomattox.

✳

exceedingly   very, to a great degree

excessively   too, too much

It's obvious from her conversation that she is *exceedingly* intelligent.

President Taft was *excessively* fat, as the photographs show.

✳

farther   more distant, in a literal sense

further   to a greater degree, in a figurative sense

Some dictionaries don't make this distinction, but I think it's worthwhile.

This tour goes *farther* into sub-Saharan Africa than the others.

I suggest, for *further* reading on Japanese culture and customs, *The Kimono Mind* by Bernard Rudofsky.

✳

imply   to communicate indirectly; to suggest

infer   to gather or figure out

Because I asked her to shut up, are you *implying* I'm rude?

From the dismal figures, I *infer* WackoToys is bankrupt.

✴

ingenious   clever, resourceful

ingenuous   naïve, innocent

Maude built an *ingenious* contraption for getting the water up the hill.

His *ingenuous* reply convinced me he knew nothing of the affair.

✴

lie   to lie down

I lie; I lay; I have lain; lying

lay   to put something down

I lay; I laid; I have laid; laying

I'm sorry to say a lot of people get these verbs confused. I know a sweet young physical therapist who says, "Just lay down on the table." I grit my teeth and comply, but I'm not happy. The sentence is incorrect and ungrammatical. It's *lie down*. The verb *to lie* doesn't take an object—a person or thing that is done to. In other words, you don't *lie* a dish, or a book, or a bag of groceries.

To lie: This is the verb to use if you are writing about getting into bed, flattening yourself on a yoga mat, or going horizontal at the beach.

I don't dare *lie* down before dinner because I'm sure to fall asleep.

He *lay* on the floor, his leg grotesquely bent.

> **Get It Right Every Time**
>
> It's confusing. The verbs *to lie* and *to lay* are obviously related, both dealing with a person or thing getting down, as it were. To make matters worse, *I lay* is the past form of *to lie* (*I lay down yesterday*) and the present form of *to lay* (*Now I lay me down to sleep*). But you'll always get it right if you remember this:
>
> **If something is being *let go of,* the correct word is *lay.* Otherwise, it's *lie.***

Marcy *has lain* there for two days. Don't you think it's time someone took her away?

Lying (not *laying*) on the sofa, Rhett overheard Scarlett's tantrum with amusement.

Just lying there, in other words, not doing anything to another person or object. You can't point to a single thing in that last sentence that Rhett is lying: He's not lying the sofa, nor Scarlett, nor her tantrum.

To lay: This is what you do with the dish, book, and bag of groceries above. You must write *I lay, I laid, I have laid*, or *laying* when you are **letting go of something**.

Tell the president he is supposed to *lay the wreath* on the Unknown Soldier's grave.

I *laid my pencil* down and took a break.

I *have laid the tile* in the upstairs bathroom.

Laying a wreath, a pencil, tile—*lay* is the right verb if you can point to something in the sentence that's being *done to*.

✳

literally	in fact; truly
figuratively	in a metaphoric, not literal, sense

Molasses was *literally* running in the gutters of Boston in 1919.

Figuratively speaking, the bill is dead as a dodo.

If you say, "I'm *buried* in paperwork," you're speaking figuratively: You are not really and truly buried. Do not mix these two words up, or use *literally* as a synonym for *thoroughly*. If you say, for example, "I was *literally* sweating bullets," your hearers will think you are a figurative nut.

✳

may	linking verb used in the present or future
might	linking verb used for the past tense

I *may* have shingles. If I don't have it now, I *may* get it.

He said she *might* have shingles.

Don't mix up your tenses by writing, "Robin Hood *vanished* into Sherwood Forest, but the villagers knew he *may* come back." If it's the villagers *knew*, it's *might*. If it's the villagers *know*, it's *may*.

Might may be used in the present, however, if you are implying doubt.

Joan says she *might* come, but only if the baby's temperature is normal.

✳

mélange	a mixture of people, places or things; an assortment, maybe of dissimilar things
ménage	household, domestic arrangement

My favorite Mrs. Malaprop (a fictional lady who made such mistakes as "I was putrefied with fear") never fails to confuse these two nice French words. If you're going to use them, be sure you've got the right one.

A *mélange* of artists, politicians, and ad copy writers had gathered in the foyer, arguing about fundraising for Venice.

Loud argument and even airborne projectiles were featured in the Clinton *ménage* when the Monica Lewinsky story hit the newsstands.

✳

militate	to operate (against)
mitigate	to lessen

Her kind nature *militates* against the evidence she is a murderer.

James's thoughtfulness *mitigated* the misery of the long wait.

✳

partially	not entirely or completely; still in process
partly	in part

Haskins is living in a *partially* renovated townhouse.

The pyramid is made *partly* of sandstone.

✳

pedal	to ride a bicycle or other transportation device by pushing the pedals
peddle	to sell or try to sell; to hawk

It's hard *pedaling* up Afton Mountain after a hefty lunch.

She was tired of *peddling* beauty products to bored housewives.

✳

principal, n.	head of school; capital, as distinct from interest; leading figure
principal, adj.	primary, major
principle, n.	abiding truth or rule

One more word and you're going to the *principal!*

The Lowells spend interest, but never *principal.*

The *principal* of the law firm is my uncle.

My *principal* reason for refusing is that I am committed that week.

She refuses to give in on *principle*, although she knows she has lost.

If it helps, I've often heard "The princi*pal* is your pal." It doesn't help me; it makes me nervous. I remember it this way: The last two syllables of *principle* are the same as *disciple*, and Jesus' disciples were men of *principle*. Everything else is *principal*. Everything.

✳

select	choice, special
selected	picked out, chosen

The advertising industry wants to blur the distinction; don't follow their lead.

A *select* group of artists will work on the Saltwater Shells mural.

This offer is available on *selected* PCs.

✳

serve	to wait upon; to take care of; to attend to
service	to maintain, as a car; to have sexual relations with (as bulls service cows)

A concierge is available in the lobby to *serve* your needs.

He needs to have the pickup truck *serviced* before the long trip.

I believe "servicing loans" is respectable usage for banks. But I have consulted for a couple of banks whose marketing materials were full of "servicing customers." I couldn't decide whether the customers were cars or cows. Say *serve*—please. Some dictionaries, it's true, allow *service* for *serve*, but to well-informed people it sounds silly and inaccurate.

✳

their	belonging to them
there	in that place; also used in "there is" and "there are"
they're	a contraction of *they are*

Mr. Schultz arranged to have *their* few possessions moved to his storage unit.

There is no reason you can't put the table over *there*.

Those aren't Clare's clown shoes; *they're* Judy's.

These are **homonyms**, words that sound exactly alike but have different meanings. Don't expect your spell or grammar checker to flag homonym mistakes reliably. In fact mine flagged "They're isn't any difference between us" (which I was considering for the exercises at the end of this chapter), inexplicably complaining that there was an extra word in "They're isn't" and suggesting "Theyisn't" instead. Sigh.

✳

Be intensely wary of the following words. Dictionaries don't admit them, term them "chiefly dialect" or "variant," or suggest they be used in speech or "informal prose" only. That's the kind of faint praise you can take as a warning. "Chiefly dialect" is code for "the speech of someone who hunts small rodents while wearing a coonskin cap." Maybe in another hundred years these words will have attained respectability. In the meantime, I would never, ever use any of them.

Untouchables	
alot	(a lot)
alright	(all right)
anyways	(anyway)
goodby	(goodbye)
heighth	(height)
irregardless	(regardless)
nother	(a whole *nother*—write *another whole*)
regards	(in the phrase *in regards to*—it's *in regard to*)
irrevelant	(irrelevant)

A young friend of mine contributed *theirchother* to this list, meaning roughly *each other*, as in "They were in love with theirchother." Kind of endearing, if not dictionary bound.

MAKE SURE YOU'VE GOT IT!

I hope you're clear on the distinctions between the word pairs and wouldn't touch the untouchables with a barge pole. Choose the correct word in parentheses and correct the untouchables wherever you find them.

1. Henry was much (*affected, effected*) by the lovely church service.
2. Please tell me how I can help. I'm here to (*serve, service*) you regardless of whether you were invited or not.
3. The (*continual, continuous*) drone of the plane's engine always puts me to sleep.
4. Sally came up with an (*ingenious, ingenuous*) method for keeping the piecrust crisp in the humid Seattle air.
5. I realize you think you saw a UFO, but here's a (*credulous, credible*) explanation.
6. Because of his skill with people, he has been (*compared to, compared with*) Ronald Reagan.
7. Mr. Gibbons was raised (*partially, partly*) in Indiana, (*partially, partly*) in Nebraska.
8. Hearing the waltzes of Johann Strauss (*evokes, invokes*) miserable hours at Arthur Murray for me.
9. He will call for us at 5:30 so that we (*may, might*) be in plenty of time for *Annie*.
10. The house was (*ensured, insured*) for $2 million at the heighth of the real estate boom.
11. Assigned seating (*militates, mitigates*) against the spirit of the reunion.
12. My (*principal, principle*) objection is that yak bones are ugly.
13. I need stocks: My portfolio is (*exceedingly, excessively*) weighted toward bonds

14. Not everything is on sale, but (*select, selected*) items are 20 percent off this week.

15. From the heads on your wall, I (*imply, infer*) your grandfather liked to shoot things.

16. The wording of the will is (*ambiguous, ambivalent*). Is the money to go to the nephew or the parakeet, and is this alright with the attorneys?

17. Do you think a new president can (*affect, effect*) the changes we need?

18. A (*discreet, discrete*) autobiography will ignore alot of your bad behavior.

19. After graduating from law school, he became (*council, counsel*) for IBM.

20. Alex's gregariousness (*complements, compliments*) his wife Sybil's intelligent and rather quiet personality.

21. (*Their, There, They're*) may be some peanuts left over from (*their, there, they're*) last party, but (*their, there, they're*) probably stale.

22. Danny looks (*as, like, as if, such as*) he could use a shoulder to cry on.

23. (*As, Like*) you promised, the bus is right on time.

24. When Jo (*lay, laid*) down at the beach, I saw her leopard tattoo.

Answer Key

1. Henry was much *affected* by the lovely church service.

2. Please tell me how I can help. I'm here to *serve* you regardless of whether you were invited or not.

3. The *continuous* drone of the plane's engine always puts me to sleep.

4. Sally came up with an *ingenious* method for keeping the piecrust crisp in the humid Seattle air.

5. I realize you think you saw a UFO, but here's a *credible* explanation.

6. Because of his skill with people, he has been *compared to* Ronald Reagan.

7. Mr. Gibbons was raised *partly* in Indiana, *partly* in Nebraska.

8. Hearing the waltzes of Johann Strauss *evokes* miserable hours at Arthur Murray for me.

9. He will call for us at 5:30 so that we *may* be in plenty of time for *Annie*.

10. The house was *insured* for $2 million at the *height* of the real estate boom.

11. Assigned seating *militates* against the spirit of the reunion.

12. My *principal* objection is that yak bones are ugly.

13. I need stocks: My portfolio is *excessively* weighted toward bonds.

14. Not everything is on sale, but *selected* items are 20 percent off this week.

15. From the heads on your wall, I *infer* your grandfather liked to shoot things.

16. The wording of the will is *ambiguous.* Is the money to go to the nephew or the parakeet, and is this *all right* with the attorneys?

17. Do you think a new president can *effect* the changes we need?

18. A *discreet* autobiography will ignore *a lot* of your bad behavior.

19. After graduating from law school, he became *counsel* for IBM.

20. Alex's gregariousness *complements* his wife Sybil's intelligent and rather quiet personality.

21. *There* may be some peanuts left over from *their* last party, but *they're* probably stale.

22. Danny looks *as if* he could use a shoulder to cry on.

23. *As* you promised, the bus is right on time.

24. When Jo *lay* down at the beach, I saw her leopard tattoo.

11

Single or Split?
Word Pairs Not to Be Confused

Don't confuse these: Just because you see *may* and *be* side by side in your sentence doesn't mean you should fuse them into *maybe*.

all together   as one; united

altogether   completely; entirely

    Let's try the chorus *all together*.

    That was *altogether* unnecessary.

✳

any one   any; any at all

anyone   any person; anybody

    I could use *any one* of these boxes for the mail.

    I couldn't make *anyone* hear me.

✳

any time   whenever

anytime   at any time whatsoever

    I can take you *any time* you need to go to the bank

    I can meet you *anytime*.

✳

common sense   practical ability (n.)

commonsense   sensible (adj.)

    She left school in the eighth grade but has a lot of *common sense*.

    Because it was raining, he chose the *commonsense* alternative of taking the train.

✳

in to	when *to* is a preposition or an infinitive
into	describes movement or change; interested in

Come *in to* New York next week.

Come *in to* see the new wallpaper.

Adele walked *into* the building.

I'm going to turn you *into* a goon.

I'm *into* all types of music except jazz.

✳

know how	to understand the method (v.)
knowhow	practical ability (n.)

I *know how* to tie some wicked knots.

Knowhow and a little luck will see us through.

✳

may be	could happen; is possibly
maybe	perhaps

Vegetarianism *may be* the best solution.

Maybe you could pick me up after work.

✳

on to	as with *into*, when *to* is a preposition or an infinitive
onto	describes movement; on top of

Come *on to* McDonald's with us afterward.

He went *on to* become a surgeon.

Bud jumped *onto* the runaway wheelchair.

✳

some time	an amount of time
sometime	one of these days; at an unspecified time

I need *some time*.

It was *some time* ago.

I'll see you *sometime* tomorrow.

*

up on	describes movement onto; well-informed about
upon	on

Jack climbed *up on* the chair.

I'm not really *up on* nanotechnology.

The fat cat sat *upon* the mat.

MAKE SURE YOU'VE GOT IT!

Correct wrong usage in the following sentences if necessary.

1. Jane has about enough commonsense to come in out of the rain.

2. He wasn't upon foreign films, but she admired his knowhow with the DVD player.

3. Isn't any one going to try to help her up on the armoire?

4. This was an all together ghastly picnic.

5. I bought a common sense guide to building a ferro-cement boat. Let's try it some time.

6. It may be too hard for Charlie to photograph us all together over the weekend.

7. Sometime I'd love to visit the Lake District and spend sometime there.

8. If you knowhow, you can do the Cossack dance, but Joan sprained her ankle trying.

9. He stepped on to the escalator, but his suitcase caught and he fell backward on to it.

10. Let's spend some time together while Roger is out of town.

11. Anytime you're feeling blue, just call me.

12. Don't touch anyone of those jellyfish.

13. That little boy went onto become Albert Einstein.

14. I'm in to Spanish. Did you know "alcatraz" means "pelican"?

Answer Key

1. Jane has about enough *common sense* to come in out of the rain.

2. He wasn't *up on* foreign films, but she admired his knowhow with the DVD player.

3. Isn't *anyone* going to try to help her up on the armoire?

4. This was an *altogether* ghastly picnic.

5. I bought a *commonsense* guide to building a ferro-cement boat. Let's try it *sometime.*

6. It may be too hard for Charlie to photograph us all together over the weekend. CORRECT AS WRITTEN

7. Sometime I'd love to visit the Lake District and spend *some time* there.

8. If you *know how,* you can do the Cossack dance, but Joan sprained her ankle trying.

9. He stepped *onto* the escalator, but his suitcase caught and he fell backward *onto* it.

10. Let's spend some time together while Roger is out of town. CORRECT AS WRITTEN

11. *Any time* you're feeling blue, just call me.

12. Don't touch *any one* of those jellyfish.

13. That little boy went *on to* become Albert Einstein.

14. I'm *into* Spanish. Did you know "alcatraz" means "pelican"?

Tone:
A Melody in the Right Key

Many things contribute to good writing: basic grammar, good control of such mechanics as punctuation or capital letters, and appearance. But none is more important than the *tone* of your e-message or letter, because it has a tremendous influence on how the reader feels about you—and therefore about your communication. The wrong tone can ruin your piece, so it's key to your success as a writer. Let's look at some ways to control tone.

Unless You're Writing Close Friends, Be Careful and Correct

If you're e-mailing a friend, I'm sure you know how to do it. On the other hand, if you're answering a job ad on Craigslist, writing a follow-up note after an interview, or sending a thank-you note to someone you don't know well, you'd be well advised to write in a fairly formal manner. I'm not trying to stifle your creativity or enthusiasm; I'm just advocating common sense. You can relax with these people later (after you get the job).

✳ **Use dignified vocabulary choices.** Watch the slang—above all tired slang:

wicked good skills	a real downer	don't dis it
a gnarly vibe	later, dude	I got chewed out

Don't include the super-informal language you use at home or with friends. Don't use abbreviations. Don't sign off with ATB for "all the best," for example. If you're e-mailing, this goes double for emoticons. Decorating with smiley faces is not in. Of *course* you wouldn't do any of these things. But it happens, and the people who matter aren't impressed.

❋ **Avoid stilted phrases.** Don't, in your eagerness to write elegantly, fall into the trap of trying to impress with strained or outdated language. Leave the following phrases and anything similar to them permanently out of your writing:

inasmuch as	enclosed please find
I beg to inform	as of even date
I remain yours truly	herewith, herein
please remit	I deem

❋ **Be straightforward and to the point.** Don't include lengthy anecdotes about yourself or anyone else. And if it's business correspondence, don't try humor. You don't know who besides your intended recipient will see your writing: someone who doesn't have the necessary context, someone with no sense of humor, or someone who just doesn't get it.

❋ **Don't pile on the clichés.** We all use clichés. They became clichés by virtue of expressing a fact or feeling especially well. But through time they've been used so hard they've gotten worn out and lost their power to command attention. Clichés are the stuff that happens when you write without thinking.

> It's plain to see our game plan is a lost cause.
>
> I'm a basket case in every way, shape, and form since Juno cut and ran on me.
>
> My heart skipped a beat until I saw Lee was walking on air and knew the plan had gone according to Hoyle.

It's not so much that clichés are wrong; it's just that there's not much right with them. You don't create a memorable impression of yourself or your ideas when you write this way. So beware of such tired language as the above, and the following:

my main squeeze	easy as falling off a log
plain as the nose on your face	first and foremost; last but not least
to the nth degree	beats the heck out of me, Chief
have a bone to pick	light at the end of the tunnel

That was easy! The little suckers just came flying off my pen because they're so familiar, and you know what familiarity breeds. See if you can't find a more original, even unforgettable, way of expressing your thoughts, or at least cut back on the clichés.

Minimize Your IQ (Insult Quotient)

This is not the kind of IQ that gets you into Harvard. I'm talking about your Insult Quotient. Writing in such a manner as to offend people or hurt their feelings won't get you in *any-where*. It's the opposite of persuasion, which brings people over to your side. If you insult people, they recoil from you and what you have to say. So beware of writing that intentionally or accidentally does the following:

✴ **Belittles the reader.**

> Most people by age 40 have been to Europe many times.

> Our customers do not generally complain about our service.

> Kindly return the jacket I lent you.

Why does the word *kindly* sound so unkind? It's amazingly down-putting. I would never use it unless I felt angry, mean, and justified and, more important, was in a position to give a zap to my correspondent without undue consequences.

✴ **Questions the reader's intelligence or competence.**

> As everybody knows, the Registry is closed at noon for lunch.

> If you will read the instruction sheet, the procedure will be perfectly clear to you.

> You should never have tried to use the hairdryer on the insulation!

Yes, even if the reader would do us all a service by hopping right out of the gene pool.

✴ **Insinuates that the reader is misinformed or, worse, lying.**

> Please be aware that it is *not* our policy to give cash refunds.

> If, as you say, you had sent me a birthday present, I certainly would have written you immediately.

> Since you supposedly warned Howard not to call Maude again, I'm astonished that he has phoned her three times.

❋ **Makes generalizations that could be hurtful to people or groups.**

> Most engineers aren't interested in art or literature.
>
> College graduates make the best personal assistants.
>
> Tall guys are usually better looking as well.

(For every tall guy who's flattered by that comment, there are five guys ready to hit the writer in the kneecap.)

❋ **Makes assumptions about gender or includes gender-related insults.**

> The daycare provider must be licensed, and *she* must be willing to relocate.
>
> When a person looks at history, *he* realizes we repeat our mistakes.
>
> Alex is a *male nurse*; Shannon is a *female lawyer*.
>
> The *men* in the office expect the *girls* to make the coffee.

If you call them *men*, call their coworkers *women*. Incidentally, some women don't like to be referred to as guys. Think they're being too sensitive? Let's try a little consciousness-raising exercise: Imagine how men would feel if we referred to them as gals. Questions? I didn't think so. The chart on page 120 shows some sexist language, with updated equivalents.

❋ **Attempts to be gender-blind by committing grammatical errors.** We won't completely solve the gender conundrum until we accept a neutral third-person single pronoun that will substitute for the tedious *he or she, him or her, his or hers*, and to date we haven't come up with one that people like. I mentioned in Chapter 2 that *s/he* is distracting, alternating *he* and *she* worse. But none of these tops the shameless wrongdoing of writing *they* or *them* instead.

Old Language	21st-Century Language
businessman	businessperson, business owner
chairman	chair
fireman	firefighter
postman	mail carrier
repairman	service rep, service technician
salesman	sales rep, salesperson
men working	work in progress
mankind	the human race
manpower	resources

No: Can a person be blamed if *they* are clumsy with heavy sculptures?

No: If you don't like your roommate, take stealthy steps to get *them* expelled.

A person or roommate is not *they*. And although the usage may come from a good place—the wish to be inclusive, not sexist—it is an ugly error.

❋ Implies that all people are Caucasian.

This movie is so scary you'll be *white as a sheet* when you come out.

The senior class is *tickled pink* that Al Gore is speaking at commencement.

Not everyone turns white when they're frightened or pink when they're pleased.

Dodging the Twin Traps of Sexism and Bad Grammar

No: When *a person* turns 18, *they are* eligible to vote.

Fixes:

Second person (*you*): When *you* turn 18, *you* are eligible to vote.

Plural: When *people* turn 18, *they* are eligible to vote.

Rewrite: Turning 18 makes a person eligible to vote.

❋ **Uses names or labels certain racial groups find offensive.** Be on guard against racial or ethnic labels that could hurt. Here are the names most Americans don't find offensive and for the most part prefer:

For people of African descent	African-American
For people of Asian descent	Asian-American
For people of Caribbean descent	Caribbean-American
For people of Latin descent	Latino
For people of Spanish or Mexican descent	Hispanic (Some Mexican people prefer Chicano; some don't like it.)
People of indigenous American descent	Native American or Native American Indian

❋ **Labels people by age.** Avoid the following: kids, tweens, teens, elders, seniors, senior citizens, the aged.

And be careful about offering anyone the senior citizen discount, especially if the person is with someone who looks younger. If senior citizens want it, they'll ask for it.

Edit "Sound Effects" Out of Your Writing

Read what you write aloud or to yourself. Remember that most readers "hear" what they're reading. Watch out for alliteration, the repetition of the same sound at the beginning of several consecutive words. Be careful that your words don't rhyme or scan, unless you're writing poetry. Don't make your prose sound absurd by committing such tuneful offenses as the following:

Dorabelle dazzled her daughter's detractors.

Sharon sampled the steak but skipped the stew.

I can't explain Jane's pain.

How did the dowager endow the town?

✳ IN BRIEF

> ⟩ Unless you're writing close friends, be careful and correct.

> ⟩ Minimize your IQ (Insult Quotient).

> ⟩ Edit "sound effects" out of your writing.

MAKE SURE YOU'VE GOT IT!

Identify the poor elements of tone in the following sentences:

1. I look forward to meeting some smart businessmen at the symposium.
2. What don't you understand about these simple instructions?
3. If I tell Estelle, Lucille will rebel.
4. I have met your so-called colleague.
5. Most football players aren't too bright.
6. My brother is marrying the cutest little Oriental girl from San Francisco.
7. Abe is old as the hills, but he's the salt of the earth.
8. Postmen in our town usually deliver the mail by noon.
9. As a senior citizen, you're probably worried about your IRAs.
10. Hiram hasn't a hope of hiring a housekeeper.

Answer Key

1. I look forward to meeting some smart businessmen at the symposium. *Who says they're men?*
2. What don't you understand about these simple instructions? *This is a classic put-down.*
3. If I tell Estelle, Lucille will rebel. *Watch out for rhyming unintentionally.*
4. I have met your so-called colleague. *This implies that the reader is lying.*
5. Most football players aren't too bright. *This sweeping generalization is bound to offend.*

6. My brother is marrying the cutest little Oriental girl from San Francisco. *Um, where to begin? This sentence is sexist, racist, and patronizing.*

7. Abe is old as the hills, but he's the salt of the earth. *Watch the pileup of clichés.*

8. Postmen in our town usually deliver the mail by noon. *Postmen isn't gender-blind.*

9. As a senior citizen, you're probably worried about your IRAs. *Don't make a point of someone's age.*

10. Hiram hasn't a hope of hiring a housekeeper. *Avoid accidental alliteration. (Joke!)*

13

Good and Bad Repetition: Rhetorical, Yes; Redundant, No

You've probably been encouraged to trim your writing by using fewer words. In many cases, this applies to the habit of repeating yourself unnecessarily and is excellent advice. We'll talk about that in the second half of this chapter. Leading with my good news, however, I'm first going to highlight the excellent uses you can make of repetition.

Use Repetition to Reinforce Your Message

Writers have used it to enhance their copy since before the time of Jesus, and it continues to be a very effective tool today.

Does anyone think the Beatles were wordy? Yet the words *let it be* appear in the song of that name an impressive 36 times. The line has *rhetorical* power: The repetition yields a sound that rings memorably in your head.

But assuming you aren't going to sing your next bit of writing, how can this help you? Here's another example:

Somewhat less effective—Churchill's famous speech as PowerPoint presentation ...

Places we shall fight them:
- beaches
- landing grounds
- fields
- streets
- hills

We shall fight them on the beaches; we shall fight on the landing grounds; we shall fight on the fields and in the streets; we shall fight on the hills; we shall never surrender.

That's Winston Churchill, whose passionate speeches stirred and cheered his fellow Englishmen during World War II. Churchill repeats *we shall fight* intentionally and effectively. Your ear responds to the words almost as if they were poetry. (Even if you don't like poetry, you'll grant it has stirring and cheering power.)

The rhetorical device of repetition is a natural if you're doing creative writing, but you can use it effectively in an environmental report, too.

> By 1970, the results of spraying pesticides in the Whitehead Valley area were obvious.

> No longer was the chorus of birds the loudest sound in the area: Residents reported the songs were few and intermittent. No longer was the squirrel and chipmunk population a nuisance: sighting either animal had become a rare event. No longer was there an overabundance of fish in the Catamount River: One fisherman estimated a 70 percent drop in his catch over ten years.

The effect of the accumulating evidence is strengthened by the repeated phase *no longer was*.

Here's another example from J.R.R. Tolkien in *The Hobbit*:

> *Who aroused* the dragon from his slumber, I might ask? *Who obtained* of us rich goods and ample help? (italics mine)

In each example, repetition lends muscle to the writing and, by extension, the argument.

Repetition Can Aid in Clarity

It can help your readers follow your thought process, especially if your subject is complicated.

> First, fiber-optic cable offers the potential for efficient, trouble-free linkage. No other medium, including analog wire transmission, can duplicate its performance. Second, fiber-optic cable is non-invasive, an important factor to homeowners and city governments alike. Third, fiber-optic cable is remarkably inexpensive, considering its advantages.

The repeated words *fiber-optic cable* return the reader to the subject, and the repetition of the familiar series *first, second, third* reinforces the structure within the paragraph to help make the relationship of each element—and your meaning—extra clear.

Repeating a word or words is also helpful where a pronoun might be unclear.

No: I loved *Perdition*, the sequel to *The Abyss*. It is gory as all get out.

Yes: I loved *Perdition*, the sequel to *The Abyss*. *Perdition* is as gory as all get out.

This kind of repetition does readers a favor: It's as if you're putting up signposts to guide them through your text. People who have to do a lot of reading will appreciate the help.

Repetition Avoids Contrived Synonyms

If it's Antarctica, don't call it the "Southernmost Continental Landmass." Call it Antarctica. Southernmost Continental Landmass looks show-offy and stuffy. Besides, it takes a lot of words. Some people, perhaps trying to ratchet up the elegance of their prose, waste time devising synonyms for terms they would otherwise be repeating.

Why should you say no to this urge? Three good reasons. First, it's often hard: There's a reason why your word of first choice *was* your first choice. Second, it is frankly not helpful, and can even be confusing, to keep encountering synonyms, especially for something that's unfamiliar (and your readers can't be expected to know everything). Third, the effort shows, and it looks beyond dumb. Consider the following:

> *The baby* woke up at the sound of the engine and began to cry. As the car sped down the road, *the newborn* continued its wailing. Irritable and edgy, the kidnappers attempted without success to calm *the neonate*, but *the chronologically challenged tiny person* kept up its lament all the way to Buffalo.

Okay, that's a little over the top. But you'd be surprised how close to such bizarre efforts even well-educated adults come. I once edited some advertising copy in which the writer referred to a bank check in a second mention as a "demand deposit advice." That's what banking folks call a check, but it mystified me, and it would have mystified the customers, too—not a good strategy.

So repetition can be very good. Why is it often bad?

Repetition Is Usually Bad When It's the Unintentional Result of Lazy Writing

Here's an example:

> I asked where the cash register was. She said the cash register was at the front of the store. I took my purchases to the cash register. The woman at the cash register rang it up.

Hello, stream of consciousness! The paragraph has a sort of sleepwalking quality to it. A less-repetitious sentence structure and a little condensing would help, with a few pronouns thrown in for good measure.

> When I asked where the cash register was, I learned it was at the front of the store. I took my purchases to the register, and the cashier rang them up.

Sometimes Repetition Equals Redundancy (Or Saying the Same Thing Twice)

This adds unnecessary bulk to your sentence and it's amateurish, if not actually incorrect. For example, here's amateurish:

> The unknown stranger's past history initially began in Communist China.

Even a moderately careful reading should make you raise your eyebrows. The sentence moves slowly and heavily because it's overburdened with unnecessary words. *Unknown, past,* and *initially* are redundant, because a stranger is by definition an unknown person, history is the past, and *began* is a synonym for *initiated*.

> The stranger's history began in Communist China.

And here's incorrect:

> First, I cut through the lobster's spinal column where the tail meets the carapace, then tested its reactions to pain, which seemed

nonexistent. When I repeated the experiment again, the other lobster also appeared to feel no pain.

Repeat means do something again. *Repeat it again* therefore means do it three times. If there were only two lobsters in all, our writer could not *repeat* the experiment *again*.

Here's a list of some common redundancies.

advance planning	join together
at this moment in time	must first be preceded
basically and fundamentally	mutual advantage of both
both…as well as	mutual cooperation
cooperate together	new innovation
consensus of opinion	other alternative
follow after	shuttle back and forth
free of charge	small in size
future projections	the reason why is because
general overview	two different kinds
inadvertent error	usual custom
in X years from now	X a.m. in the morning/evening

What's the alternative to a moment in time? A moment in space? Think about it, and don't write stupid stuff. That will depress your reader, and a depressed reader won't like *what* you've written any better than the way you wrote it. I'm a reader, and I approved this message.

✳ IN BRIEF

> Use repetition to reinforce your message.

> Repetition can aid in clarity.

> Repetition avoids contrived synonyms.

> Repetition is usually bad when it's the unintentional result of lazy writing.

> Sometimes repetition equals redundancy (or saying the same thing twice).

MAKE SURE YOU'VE GOT IT!

Decide whether the following sentences include examples of good or bad repetition, and make corrections if necessary.

1. Sandy both woke me at 4:00 a.m. in the morning as well as kept me up all night.

2. Hauser is a talented 13-year-old teenager, but I feel a biography of his life is premature.

3. Mrs. Gibbons worked at the Trinity College library in Hartford, Connecticut, for many years. Though her skills as a reference librarian were legendary, she was skilled in cataloguing as well. I'd recommend her for a position as a college librarian anywhere.

4. If we cooperate together, we can avoid these inadvertent errors.

5. I landed the fish; I removed the hook from the fish; the fish bit me; I finally lost the fish overboard.

6. I asked for a banana, and a waitress brought me the crescent-shaped yellow fruit.

7. Blessed are the pure in heart: for they shall see God. Blessed are the peacemakers: for they shall be called the children of God.

8. The general consensus of opinion was that Angel Clare was a louse.

9. Mix the butter and flour to make a roux in a saucepan while the lobster cools; add the hot milk to the roux all at once.

10. Some said a billfold containing $10,000 was plucked from the body of the pilot; others spoke of a briefcase holding twice that amount; still others said a vest with $1,500 in the pocket was floating in the cockpit.

11. My keyboard has had to go in for repair three times; I am beginning to hate my information input device.

12. In 1905, there were no rules or regulations about making money: no Securities and Exchange Commission, no Federal Reserve, no Federal Trade Commission.

13. The movie *The Gods Must Be Crazy* is a film about an African Bushman who finds a Coke bottle, which, although small in size, causes big trouble.

Answer Key

1. Sandy both woke me at 4:00 *a.m. and* kept me up all night.
2. Hauser is a talented *thirteen-year-old,* but I feel a *biography is* premature.
3. Mrs. Gibbons worked at the Trinity College library in Hartford, Connecticut, for many years. Though her skills as a reference librarian were legendary, she was skilled in cataloguing as well. I'd recommend her for a position as a college librarian anywhere. GOOD REPETITION
4. If we *cooperate,* we can avoid *these errors.*
5. I landed the fish *and* removed the hook from *it, and then it* bit me. I finally lost the fish overboard.
6. I asked for a banana, and a waitress brought me *one.*
7. Blessed are the pure in heart: for they shall see God. Blessed are the peacemakers: for they shall be called the children of God. GOOD REPETITION
8. The *consensus* was that Angel Clare was a louse.
9. Mix the butter and flour to make a roux in a saucepan while the lobster cools; add the hot milk to the roux all at once. GOOD REPETITION
10. Some said a billfold containing $10,000 was plucked from the body of the pilot; others spoke of a briefcase holding twice that amount; still others said a vest with $1,500 in the pocket was floating in the cockpit. GOOD REPETITION
11. My keyboard has had to go in for repair three times; I am beginning to hate my *keyboard.*
12. In 1905, there were no rules or regulations about making money: no Securities and Exchange Commission, no Federal Reserve, no Federal Trade Commission. GOOD REPETITION
13. The movie *The Gods Must Be Crazy* is *about* an African Bushman who finds a Coke bottle, which, although *small,* causes big trouble.

14

Scary Writing: Illogical, Mystifying, and Out of Control

As I've pointed out in several places, one of the biggest reasons for writing well is to get the reader on your side: to gain his or her confidence. If you have reader buy-in, you can express all kinds of wacky notions and readers will pay attention. But you don't get buy-in with writing that's weird or nonsensical.

In this chapter, I offer some illogical, mystifying, and out-of-control writing, with explanations and fixes.

Make Noun and Pronoun References Clear

Otherwise you risk being mystifying. For example:

> When Rob asked Joshua for the DVD, he didn't understand that he hadn't gotten permission to use it.

This sentence is correct in grammar and profoundly flawed in conveying meaning. To which lad do these *he* pronouns refer? Was it Rob who didn't understand, or Joshua? Was it Joshua or Rob who didn't have permission? If the reader already knows something about the situation, the meanings may be clear—but don't bet on it. And even if they do have some prior information, most readers don't like having to work to understand what they're reading. Remember that, when you are completely in the know, it's easy to forget that others may need very clear signals in order to understand.

Pronouns can also be misused to refer to something unclear or hazy:

> I tried to dig my way out of my terrible situation on the steep, avalanche-prone mountain, but *it* was just too heavy and wet for me.

> We may not at first realize what J.D. Salinger's hero Holden Caulfield is
> doing, but if you've ever taken a Psych course you'll identify *it* as
> depression.

The pronoun *it* is the culprit in both sentences. In the first,
it refers to nothing in the sentence that we can name, and that's
not good. Pronouns must have antecedents. Was the terrible situation heavy and wet? The mountain? We can guess the writer
means some heavy, wet snow, but guessing isn't good enough.
You need to put the snow in there somewhere. The sentence is
imprecise as it stands.

In the second example, *it* refers to what Holden Caulfield is
doing, and you don't *do* depression. You can do work, or a paper,
or lunch, but it's not idiomatic English to write that someone's
doing depression. At least not yet. (Not now, please—I'm doing
depression at least until this afternoon....)

> Jen is a *cheerleader, an activity* I doubt I'll ever try.

What's wrong here? We get the idea, but the sentence structure is poor because a *cheerleader* is not an *activity*. The noun
activity must exactly describe something in the first part of the
sentence. When your reference is inexact, as this one is, readers
may not be sure what's wrong, but it makes them uneasy. You
could write the following:

> Jen is into cheerleading, an activity I doubt I'll ever try.

OR

> Jen is a cheerleader, something I doubt I'll ever be.

OR

> Jen is a cheerleader, a peppy person I would deeply dislike to be.

Here's another:

> I can't live without my iPod, and the really tiny new one is my goal.

Sorry—although again you can grasp what this person is saying, it's bad writing. A piece of equipment, however cherished, is
not a goal. Say instead:

> I can't live without my iPod, and my goal is to own one of the really
> tiny new ones.

Don't Mix Metaphors

You may recall from poetry class that a metaphor is a way of describing something by likening it to something else. It's different from a simile—*she is like a swan*, for example—because it doesn't use the word like, but rather describes something in terms of something else. *The ship plowed through the waves*, for example, describes the motion of the ship by comparing it to a plow, which turns earth in a field. *Rick held court as all the girls rushed to sit near him* compares a young man to a king ruling his subjects.

"She's a witch who flocks to lasso every new kid on the block."

Trouble sneaks in when you mix two or more metaphors that conflict.

> She's a witch who flocks to lasso every new kid on the block.

Ooo-kay. So is she a witch, a sheep, or a cowgirl? The writer should have decided on one and done some judicious pruning.

> She's a witch who puts a spell on every new kid on the block.

At least this fix is less complex. Next, look at this pileup:

> I'd love to help pull your chestnuts out of the lions' den, but I'm running on empty without a safety net.

At least stick with the usual form of a metaphor. In the preceding sentence, the traditional phrase is *to pull someone's chestnuts out of the fire*. *The lions' den* belongs in its own metaphor—it's a reference to the arena into which early Christians were flung with hungry lions to satisfy the Romans' taste for spectacle. Together, the two metaphors spin quickly out of control.

And *running on empty* is a gas-tank metaphor to indicate depletion or exhaustion. Mixed with the net of a high-wire circus act, it creates the picture of a car tumbling into a net, with predictably disastrous results. Simplify:

✳ 133

I'd love to help you with your problem, but I'm running on empty myself and haven't any extra cash [or whatever].

You become ineffective as well as silly when you mix metaphors, because they distract from your message and make your prose difficult to understand.

> **What's the Problem?**
>
> Humor is fine in its place; unintentional humor is deadly to your image as a competent writer. Don't risk it by writing humorous prose, heaven forbid, by accident!

Don't Allow Dangling Participles or Misplaced Modifiers in Your Writing

A dangling participle is a fancy word for a simple concept. Participles are usually *–ing* words expressing a verb in the present tense: eating, copying, dealing, wondering. They are often part of a phrase at the beginning of a sentence.

> *Cursing* the knight who had defeated him, the monster writhed, then lay still.

> *Glittering* in the late afternoon sun, the lake was a sheet of burnished gold.

> *Kicking* over the lantern, the cow became an arsonist.

Please note in each of these cases, the next noun in the sentence— the subject of the main sentence itself, which follows the introductory phrase—tells who or what was, you should pardon the expression, – *inging*: The monster was cursing, the lake glittering, the cow kicking. That's fine. Trouble comes in when a writer decides to follow the phrase with something that is *not* the subject of the clause.

"Sneaking into my bedroom very late, my shoes squeaked and woke Mom."

> Sneaking into my bedroom very late, my shoes squeaked and woke Mom.

134 ✳

No, no, no. It wasn't the shoes that were sneaking. Even if they were sneakers.

> Tearing around the corner at 60 mph, 90-year-old Mrs. Moffett was right in the middle of the road.

Now it surely wasn't Mrs. M at her advanced age who tore around the corner at 60. We're missing the doer of the action: a truck, a car, a person driving a truck or a car.

> Tearing around the corner at 60 mph, the driver saw 90-year-old Mrs. Moffett right in the middle of the road.

> As the car tore around the corner at 60 mph, 90-year-old Mrs. Moffett was right in the middle of the road.

Do you see? The **very next thing** that follows the *–ing* phrase needs to be what the phrase is describing. Or you must include the doer of the action in the first phrase.

A participle can end in *-ed*, too, as in this unfortunate sentence:

> Dressed in an orange satin pantsuit and white gloves, I immediately recognized Michael Jackson.

The subject of the main sentence is *I*, so the *dressed* clause gloms right onto it: This writer has said he or she was dressed in an orange satin pantsuit and white gloves. Knowing Michael Jackson as we do, we may be pretty sure *he* was the one with the wardrobe problem, but that's not what the sentence is saying. You can easily fix the sentence in many ways.

> Dressed in an orange satin pantsuit and white gloves, Michael Jackson was immediately recognizable.

In the following sentence, there's no telltale *–ing* or even *–ed* word to prompt revising, but it's saying something very peculiar:

> A child of the '60s, Charles Dickens did not appeal to him.

It's saying, in fact, that Dickens was a flower child.

Here's another:

> With the fanatical rage and humorless countenance of a Puritan, I watched Eliot Spitzer terrorize Wall Street.

Would you talk that way about yourself? Our writer, surely by accident, did exactly that. That modifying clause grabs right onto what it understandably takes to be the subject of the sentence: *I*.

Don't serve your readers this kind of thing. Of course they'll lose confidence in your writing and begin to question what you write. Those sentences could have read this way:

> A child of the '60s, he found Charles Dickens unappealing.

> With the fanatical rage and humorless countenance of a Puritan, Eliot Spitzer terrorized Wall Street.

Remove "You've Got to Be Kidding" Statements

Readers will most definitely lose confidence in your content if your prose inspires them to say, "You've got to be kidding." Don't push them in that direction with writing such as this. I'm quoting from a feature in a major daily newspaper:

> Minorities are sorely represented in the [XYZ] Registry.

I know what *sorely underrepresented* means, but whatever did this writer have in mind? I first saw the sentence a while back: It's taken me weeks to realize that possibly the writer meant *poorly represented*. Sorely is pretty close to poorly, but close isn't good enough. Same paper, different date:

> The Black Hawk chopper was downed in by a missile.

Downed, maybe, or *done in by a missile*, but *downed in*? More than the helicopter is out of control here.

I kind of enjoy reading the goofs people make—but I wouldn't want to be the one making them. Read very carefully before you print to be certain you haven't committed any of these mistakes.

✳ IN BRIEF

≫ Make noun and pronoun references clear.

≫ Don't mix metaphors.

≫ Don't allow dangling participles or misplaced modifiers in your writing.

≫ Remove "You've got to be kidding" statements.

MAKE SURE YOU'VE GOT IT!

Spot the errors and try your hand at correcting them. Your fixes may be different from the answers here, but never mind: The important thing is to identify what's wrong.

1. Working feverishly in order to take Veterans' Day off, my computer died in the middle of my article on gardening with children.
2. June told Kirsten she was the target of malicious gossip.
3. Brett loves those Sudoku puzzles, but it isn't my idea of fun.
4. The surfer plowed through the water searching for the Holy Grail of waves.
5. He doesn't strike much of a figure as a leader.
6. Dancing at the Purple Persimmon, my tights had a huge rip in them.
7. Keith held Jonathan's head under water. He punched him in the stomach.
8. Nate spends all his time mountaineering, something I'll never be.
9. Presented as a work of fiction, her editors are thrilled at the book's reception.
10. Her eyes locked onto his, boring into them like deep forest pools.
11. The fiddleheads are past being edible to pick.
12. Extensive coffee-drinking has been shown to reduce diabetes in men, which is an interesting area of study.
13. All clothing must be removed from your closet for a thorough cockroach spraying.

Answer Key

1. *I was working* feverishly in order to take Veterans' Day off *when* my computer died in the middle of my article on gardening with children.
2. June told Kirsten *that she, Kirsten,* was the target of malicious gossip.

✳ 137

3. Brett loves *working* Sudoku puzzles, but it isn't my idea of fun.

4. The surfer plowed through the water *looking for the ultimate wave.*

5. He doesn't *cut* much of a figure as a leader.

6. Dancing at the Purple Persimmon, *I was horrified to discover a huge rip in* my tights.

7. Keith held Jonathan's head under water. *Jonathan punched Keith* in the stomach.

8. Nate spends all his time mountaineering, *a sport I'll never try*.

9. Presented as a work of fiction, *the book is getting a reception that thrills the editors.*

10. Her eyes, *like deep forest pools, gazed into his.*

11. *Don't pick the fiddleheads now: They're past their prime and inedible.*

12. *An interesting area of study is the effect of extensive coffee-drinking in men, which* has been shown to reduce diabetes.

13. *Your closet must be emptied for a thorough spraying for cockroaches.*

15

Appalling Prose: Believe It or Not, This Stuff Actuallly Got Published

What could the writers of the following have been thinking when they penned these frankly appalling bloopers? These sentences would cause anyone who cares about correct writing to break out in hives. I'm including them here to remind you what a good writer you really are. At least you aren't guilty of *these*.

Appallingly Redundant
(Why Not Say It Twice to Get the Point Across?)

It's increasingly looking more and more like....

You can be rest assured....

Let's get back to the basic fundamentals.

But in this ever-changing world in which we live in....

(Sir Paul wrote it, but that doesn't make it right.)

Appallingly Close but No Cigar
(You Aren't Allowed to Make Up Your Own Idioms.)

an on-the-loose cannon

He open-fired on the crowd.

He doesn't even know French, yet alone English.

the dearly departed

As far as those statistics, we don't really know.

Appallingly Confused
(A Nasty Bunch)

The walls, no doubt once been covered with wallpaper, were painted white.

The mayor got a lot of back-lashing on that proposal.

He was waxing (not waxing eloquent or waxing floors—just sitting around waxing).

...and Xerox's good news didn't hurt just a bit.

By aggressively treating symptoms, we can result in a complete cure.

No cash exchanged hands.

Appallingly Malapropos

All of us unconsciously use *pneumonics* to help us remember things.
(The writer meant *mnemonics*, devices to aid memory; *pneumonics* would mean things related to the lungs.)

I was a social *piranha*.
(A *pariah* is someone who is ostracized or shunned. But there's no doubt people shun *piranhas* also.)

No one could *correlate* her story.
(I'm guessing *corroborate* was the word intended.)

We were on the balcony when it suddenly *gave away*.
(It was probably giving away candy: A nice effect is produced when you throw it from above.)

People disgorged from inside the building and disappeared into their cars.
(Yes, but *what* did they disgorge? Inquiring minds—well, maybe they don't want to know.)

This act is *symblematic* of her devotion to the club.
(I'm not sure of the spelling: The word is from a speech rather than a document, which is lucky.)

PART III
APPEARANCE: LOOKING GOOD IS THE BEST REVENGE

You could call the following "mechanical" issues superficial. Sure, the way shaving before a job interview is superficial. Let's face it: Appearance matters. Though capital letters, numbers, and the rest may be little things, they can weigh unduly on your sensitive reader—the one who flips through your carefully written paragraphs to see just how many times you capitalized *secretary* when you should have lowercased it. That reader isn't taking in a word you wrote. Need I say more?

16

Punctuation: On the Road

I think of punctuation as road signage to guide you through a piece of writing. A colon says **Caution**, here's an explanation, quote, or series; a dash says **Turn**, here comes a sharp break in direction; a quotation mark says **Look Out**, direct quote ahead; a period, like a red light, says **Stop**; and so on. Okay, maybe that's too cute. My point is that these little marks shouldn't be a source of worry. They're meant to be friendly and helpful. If they spook you, you probably need a review, and here it is. Please note that commas, because they're a big deal, have their own chapter (Chapter 17).

&| Ampersand

This symbol stands for *and*, and I suggest that you think twice before using it. It's been around for a long time and was liberally employed in the 18th century both in formal writing (legislature, petitions, and so forth) and in correspondence. Since that time its use has dwindled; it is now seen chiefly in firm and company names and departments.

> Crabtree & Evelyn
>
> the law firm of McCandlish & Lillard
>
> Crosse & Blackwell
>
> BankBuffalo Research & Development

Please don't use it in place of *and* in running copy, where it looks old-fashioned and odd.

No: The band uses both acoustic & electric guitars.

Yes: The band uses both acoustic and electric guitars.

Apostrophe

The apostrophe chiefly signifies possession or omission. In a few cases it is used to form a plural.

Possession

Use an apostrophe with a final *s* to signify ownership.

Nick's train   *Alex's* socks   the *United Press's* file photos

Yes, add the apostrophe even if the word ends in *x* or *s*. (For more on that, please see Chapter 8.)

Use an apostrophe to make a plural noun ending in *s* possessive.

the *Smiths'* children   the *boys'* clubhouse   the *businesses'* founders

Use an apostrophe with a final *s* if the plural noun doesn't end in *s*.

the *geese's* constant cackling

the *women's* locker room

the *people's* choice

Omission

Use an apostrophe where a letter or letters are left out. The word thus formed is called a **contraction.**

it's been a long time (a contraction of *it has*)

it's no big deal (a contraction of *it is*)

she was a big star in the *'70s* (a contraction of *1970s*)

you're right, you *should've* called (contractions of *you are* and *should have*)

att'n of the *sec'y* (contractions of *attention* and *secretary*; note they're written without periods)

The rule in *Words into Type* is that you don't use periods with contractions. As always, though, follow your organization's house style, or be consistent with your own.

Plurals

Don't overdo this one. You need a good reason to add an apostrophe with a plural *s*. If a misreading is possible—for example, with abbreviations or letters of the alphabet—add an apostrophe before the *s* when forming a plural.

The *a*'s and *m*'s on that sign aren't clear.

He revved the engine up to 3,000 *rpm*'s.

If a misreading is unlikely, nowadays the apostrophe is usually omitted.

She has her BA and two *MA*s from Tulane.

He was born in the *1920*s.

Bank of America has *ATM*s on every corner.

[|] Brackets

Always used in pairs, brackets are used to set a word, phrase, or sentence off from the rest of your material. Use brackets if you must excerpt something that falls inside parentheses.

Hitler (having overrun the Sudetenland [in present-day Czechoslovakia] the preceding September) refused to yield.

You can see it would be confusing to use parentheses inside parentheses. Think of the brackets in such a situation as second-generation parentheses.

Brackets may also be used to indicate that the writer is speaking. This is a useful device for a newspaper quoting someone who has been unclear or has used words the paper won't publish.

Wilson said, "It's a terrible place [the old Washington Street jail]. You can't get comfortable in those [awful] cells on those [lousy] mattresses stuffed with straw."

The word *sic* (*thus* in Latin), italicized, is used in brackets to indicate that a mistake in spelling, fact, whatever, isn't the writer's doing.

"He never paid me what I urned [*sic*] when I worked for him in the St. Louis office," she wrote.

[:] Colon

The colon indicates that what follows is going to be an explanation, an example, or a more detailed statement of what went before. A dash is often used instead, but the colon is the more formal mark of the two.

Peter has a problem with the concert: He says there is too much music from the Baroque period and not enough from the Romantic period. (explanation)

I've included books many people have read: *The Da Vinci Code*, for example. (example)

We need warm clothing for the refugees: coats, hats, mittens, and boots. (more detailed statement)

You may use a capital letter following a colon if what follows is a complete sentence.

I must make an unwelcome announcement: Bonuses are being suspended.

The colon also may be used to introduce a list.

The agenda for the meeting is as follows:

➤ to introduce Bob Bartley, our new secretary

➤ to get an update on the MiTech project

➤ to hear the results of Jason's research

➤ to finalize plans for the trade show

Use a colon to introduce a quotation, especially a long one.

Shakespeare's *Hamlet* soliloquy begins this way:

To be or not to be, that is the question
Whether 'tis nobler in the mind to suffer....

Turning to the waitress, Gerald said: "I've never had worse service."

A comma is correct also, particularly if the quotation is short.

Use a colon after the salutation in a letter:

Dear Sir:

Dear Madison:

> What I mean by a "long" quotation is actually a quotation in its own separate paragraph, or in lined verse. A "short" quotation would be in running copy.

The colon is increasingly preferred over a comma except in the most informal letters.

Don't interrupt a sentence with a colon.

No: Doris says she wants: her sneakers, her bathing suit, and a hat.

Yes: Doris says she wants her sneakers, her bathing suit, and a hat.

No: I announced to the group: that I had decided to resign.

Yes: I announced to the group that I had decided to resign.

The colons are unnecessary and incorrect in the previous "No" sentences. As a rule, in running copy a colon should be preceded by a complete sentence.

── Em Dash

Use an em dash (the long dash) without spaces on either side, in the following situations:

❋ **To introduce a sharp break in thought or interruption of a sentence.**

> It's very late—oh, my heavens, where on earth is Jackie?

> But Stephen—I wish you could have heard him—argued brilliantly.

❋ **To indicate that a summary or fuller statement follows, as you would a colon.**

> I need three volunteers—one to watch the door and two to punch tickets.

> The business plan is excellent—concise, well organized, and persuasive.

A dash is considered less formal than a colon, but in all but the stuffiest situations it is acceptable.

❋ **To highlight or specially emphasize an element.**

> The dancing—I can't get Eva Lypskaya's jumps out of my mind—was superb.

> If you go south—and you owe it to yourself—apply SPF twice a day.

Note that the dashes are more eye-catching than parentheses or commas and therefore make a stronger statement.

─ En Dash

Use an en dash to indicate a range. The en dash is shorter than an em dash but longer than a hyphen. Use it between pairs of numbers or dates or anything else to indicate *from x to y*: 1914–1918 signifies *from 1914 to 1918*. The en dash can mean through as well.

The assignment is to read pages *7–42* in *Becoming One with Phyllo Dough*.

Privates *MacIntosh–Peterson* will report for duty at Quonset A.

The 30 Years' War, *1618–48*, was actually a series of wars.

The meeting is scheduled *9:00 a.m.–4:30 p.m.*

Note that in page and year ranges you may omit any digits that don't change, although your second number must have at least two digits.

No: 1841-2

Yes: 1841–42

Yes: 1999–2004

⋯ Ellipsis Points

An ellipsis resembles a series of three periods and is used to signify that something has been omitted, usually in material quoted from another source.

> The Beatles...made their stunning American debut on the Ed Sullivan Show in 1966. (*The Entertainer*, May 5, 2002)

When the omitted material would have come at the end of the quote, a fourth point is included, which is the period.

> Keats writes:
>
> Love in a hut, with water and a crust,
>
> Is—Love, forgive us!—cinders, ashes, dust....

Ellipsis points can also indicate a pause or hesitation in quoted speech.

> Janet said, "I don't know whether...maybe if I could finish this proposal today...."

! Exclamation Point

Concerning this mark, it's more a question of taste than of rules. You may use an exclamation point wherever you see fit. The best advice I can give you is not to overuse it. You weaken the effect and, particularly in formal writing, may make yourself look less than serious—maybe even a little foolish.

I insist that we fire Agatha! She is so abrasive that our clients are all complaining! The situation is untenable!

You get the point. Unless you are e-mailing your best friend from high school, I suggest limiting yourself to one exclamation per written piece. All right, two. No more.

⎣-⎦ Hyphen

This is the shortest of the lateral lines and has nothing to do with the dashes. The hyphen exists for a couple of very specific purposes:

✳ **To clarify relationships between words.** This is the most important function of this mark.

> If I write *ten thousand dollar bills*, to how many bills am I referring? Ten of them, each worth one thousand dollars? Or an unspecified number of ten thousand dollar bills? Here's how each would look:
>
> ten thousand-dollar bills
>
> any number of ten-thousand-dollar bills

There's quite a difference, and it's the hyphens that are making that difference.

✳ **When a compound (two words or more) adjective precedes a noun.**

> A *well-rehearsed* cast usually does a creditable job.
>
> His first "ride" was an *eight-cylinder* Cadillac.
>
> We enjoyed LuAnn's *tongue-in-cheek* send-up of Eminem.

Be sure you include all parts of the compound in your hyphenation.

> He acts like a *three-year-old* child.

It's not *three year-old* or *three year-old child*. The hyphens make it clear that *three-year-old* is a single descriptive phrase.

Here are some examples of suspended hyphenation, which you may need to use once in a while:

> The *down-* and *feather-filled* pillows are less firm than the foam rubber ones.

Each person must decide for *him-* or *herself.*

When you compare the *second-* and *third-class* postage rates, it's clear that money can be saved.

Remember that I said "once in a while." Don't overdo it. You can usually rewrite (*down and feather pillows*), and it's not the end of the world if you repeat your root word (*second-class and third-class postage*).

Note that without hyphens in a compound before a noun, there's potential for confusion, as with the dollar bills example. Look at these two phrases, with and without a hyphen:

a fast moving truck

a fast-moving truck

The first means a truck used for moving furniture (or something else) that goes fast; the second means a regular truck—be it a Peterbilt or a Mack—that is fast. Here's another:

He has a pretty-serious girlfriend.

He has a pretty, serious girlfriend.

In the first sentence, the girlfriend is in a serious relationship; in the second, she is both pretty and serious. (Probably doesn't laugh a lot, but no one's perfect.) The hyphen makes a big difference in these sentences.

DECISIONS, DECISIONS...

The "pretty, serious" girlfriend?...   or the "pretty-serious" girlfriend?

Note that if a compound adjective phrase comes *after* the noun it describes, there is no need to hyphenate, because there is little chance of confusion.

The firm bought *over-the-counter* stock.

These holdings are stocks sold *over the counter*.

He seems a *well-intentioned* sort of fellow.

A person who is *well intentioned* may nonetheless offend.

Exceptions to the rule: You need not hyphenate after the word *very*, because it's so familiar that confusion is unlikely. Also there's usually no need to hyphenate after *–ly* adverbs, because their form indicates their position in the sentence.

> What should you do with "small business owner," a tiny person I picture at a huge desk ordering people around? To be clear, write "small-business owner" or "owner of a small business."

We have had a *very difficult* evening.

Elaine had a *wholly unexpected* encounter with Claude.

I was amazed to see a *beautifully constructed* gazebo.

❋ **Between the parts of any compound word.** And there are a lot of them. If you aren't sure of the correct form, consult your dictionary, which is amazingly helpful. It will tell you whether a compound is spelled open (*foster mother, fellow officer*) closed (*backache, bathhouse*), or hyphenated (*self-discipline, vice-regent*).

If you're sufficiently interested, the *Chicago Manual of Style*, which is fabulously useful, devotes six pages to the various categories of compound words.

❋ **To indicate division of a word at the end of a line.** Note that your dictionary and your PC tell you where to divide a word. There's no need to try to figure it out for yourself—in fact, please don't.

Three tall vases of Baccarat crystal filled with cymbidium orchids stood in the center of each table.

❋ As a substitute for *and, versus,* or *to* in constructions such as the following:

> I watched all the Nixon-Kennedy debates as a child.

> The Boston-Cincinnati flight is fully booked.

> The 1964 Ali-Liston fight "shook up the world."

Note that the name of a court case is an exception. You don't use a hyphen, and versus is abbreviated *v.*

> the case of Marbury *v.* Madison

❋ **In numbers between 21 and 99 in written-out form.**

sixty-two   five hundred seventy-five   two thousand fifty-two

?! Interrobang

I couldn't resist putting this in. Surely you've seen the mark—often on the comics page—which signifies roughly, "Can you believe it?" or "What th—?"

> Your old nemesis was elected Miss Congeniality (?!).

> Is interrobang a great word or what?!

( ) Parentheses

Use these marks to excerpt information, usually a small amount that doesn't materially affect your sentence.

> He stopped by the construction site (at Seventh and Main) only to see his brother.

> Cheryl's hip replacement (the doctor insists it's necessary) is scheduled for September 24.

> In the middle of the wedding ceremony, it is discovered (p. 217) that Mr. Rochester is already married—to a madwoman.

Never place a punctuation mark ahead of a right-facing parenthesis.

No: He's my friend, (so he says) but I don't trust him.

Yes: He's my friend (so he says), but I don't trust him.

Following are two correct ways to punctuate and capitalize with parentheses.

> Jocelyn was furious. (It showed.)

> Jocelyn was furious (it showed).

When you enclose a phrase or sentence in parentheses, as in the first example, you make a stronger break between it and the main sentence. In the second example, the parenthetical material is more closely joined to the sentence.

I prefer **not** to use parentheses if I can avoid it. If material is important enough to include, I think it should be a legitimate part of the sentence, not stuck in like some sort of poor relation. It also breaks up your sentence and makes it look choppy. You can easily incorporate the information in most parentheses into your sentence, usually as nonrestrictive material set off by commas.

> Cheryl's hip replacement, which the doctor insists is necessary, is scheduled for September 24.

> Jocelyn was furious, and it showed.

I save the marks for necessary but really not interesting material, such as *p. 217* in the Mr. Rochester example on page 152.

. Period

I like the English term, *full stop*, because it's nicely descriptive: You place a period because you have come to a full stop.

Use a Period to Indicate the End of a Sentence or Sentence Fragment

> Sally taught hot yoga classes before she became a lawyer.

> I've said all I'm going to say. That's it.

You don't need to put periods at the end of items in a vertical list unless the items are complete sentences.

> Each person will need to bring the following:
>
> foul weather gear
>
> sleeping bag
>
> pillow, if desired

In the following example each list item is a complete sentence, so periods are used.

> I've pointed out these features of Arachne:
>
> The project will bring the entire team together.
>
> No one who's not willing will be asked to work overtime.
>
> Arachne will be complete before Christmas.

Also note that the period, like the comma, always goes **inside** quotation marks, whether it is part of the quoted material or not.

> This electrifying article is entitled "Driving Your Carburetor Clean."

Read more on this phenomenon in the following section on quotation marks, and also in Chapter 17 on commas.

Use Periods With Some Abbreviations

Put periods after someone's initials and after such titles as Mr., Dr., and Esq.

> The poet *O.A.* Manning is the fictional creation of the fictional Charles Todd, actually a mother and son writing team.
>
> *Mrs.* Johnson looks as if she needs medical attention, but *Dr.* Bell's away.

Note that the custom of using periods after all letter abbreviations is changing. The National Association of Colored People, for example, was abbreviated for years as *N.A.A.C.P.*, but the organization now writes *NAACP*.

> *RPI* used to have a terrific football team.
>
> "*NASA* Scrubs Space Flight Again"
>
> He has both a *BA* and an *MA* in Victorian literature.

Make sure you follow the style of any organization whose abbreviation you're writing.

" " Quotation Marks

If you're quoting directly from spoken or written speech, using someone's exact words, enclose the quoted material within these marks.

Herb said, "You're going to have to work a lot harder on the big machines to get those quads back into shape."

"If the doorbell rings, don't answer it," she begged.

Remember that commas and periods go inside quotation marks, even if they are part of your sentence rather than the quotation. All other marks of punctuation go inside or outside, depending on whether they are part of the quoted material.

Her advice, not surprisingly, was, "Don't touch the principal"; I completely agree.

His article, "Growing Up with Huckleberry Finn," has generated a lot of interest in this small town.

In 1978, Letitia Baldwin wrote, "Polka dot napkins are being used with plaid tablecloths"!

General Pershing may not have been the one who said, "Lafayette, we are here!"

Titles of certain works should be enclosed in quotation marks: poems, magazine and newspaper articles and features, and chapters and other parts of books:

Have you read "The Yellow Wallpaper" in *The Feminist Anthology*?

"A Hometown Hero's Welcome" appeared in *The Denver Post*.

"Daddy," a poem by Sylvia Plath, uses Nazi and Fascist images.

An unfamiliar word or phrase may be set off in quotation marks.

Do you understand what "convertible debentures" are?

She referred several times to "shaken child syndrome" in her statement to the jury.

Quotation marks also may be used to indicate that something may be so called but is actually not the real McCoy.

She says the candy is "homemade," but I suspect it's from Sweet Tooth.

Be aware of this usage and don't enclose something in quotation marks, in advertising copy or elsewhere, as a way to highlight or draw attention to it.

Come in to Hector's Auto for "Big Savings"!

Not only does it look sort of retro, it casts doubt on the depth of Hector's commitment to saving his customers money. Probably accurately, too, but that's not what the writer intended.

These fish are "fresh"!

Uh oh. None for me, thanks.

; | Semicolon

This mark forms a break stronger than a comma creates but less strong than that of a period. Use it to connect two related sentences, usually without a conjunction such as *and* or *but*.

> The tide was extraordinarily high; the beach was almost gone.

> The doctor stripped vein after vein from my leg; I decided he was making another person in the back room and needed the veinage.

In most cases you must not connect two sentences with a comma. Use a semicolon instead.

No: Adele is an ideal employee, we are fortunate to have her in the office.

Yes: Adele is an ideal employee; we are fortunate to have her in the office.

Use a semicolon, not a comma, before *however*, *therefore*, and *moreover*.

No: The temperature is falling rapidly, moreover, tomorrow is supposed to be even colder.

Yes: The temperature is falling rapidly; moreover, tomorrow is supposed to be even colder.

The semicolon is also useful to mark and clarify divisions between items in a series that contains other internal punctuation.

What's the Problem?

If you don't observe the rules of punctuation, your meaning may not be clear. Correct punctuation serves as a guide to meaning.

The Open Space Committee was responsible for installing the bluebird houses, located in Robinson's Field, where conditions are almost ideal; pulling down the old barn, which had become dangerous, and removing the lumber; and creating a pond for ducks, fish, and frogs.

The picture shows Kip, the project manager, behind the desk; James, the systems analyst; Marge, the administrative assistant; and Bascom, the programmer.

You can see how easily the bits of identifying information in both these sentences could attach themselves to the wrong thing. The semicolons perform a useful function. Use them in similar situations. Remember: Your readers don't know as much as you do, so these guideposts add welcome clarification.

‹ › Single Quotation Marks

Don't use these unless you have a good reason. Their function is to enclose a title, quote, or other material that would normally be enclosed in double quotation marks, within another quote.

Stanley responded, "How can I answer your question? I have never even read 'The Solitary Reaper.'"

"The candidate doesn't have a prayer," Ronald said. "When asked about his family, he answered, 'No comment'!"

/ Slash

This is a useful mark, though it is overused and sometimes misused. Joining two words or phrases, it means "either or both."

The tourists use buses/taxis to get around the city.

This is an efficient way of expressing a wordier concept: Some tourists are using buses, some are using taxis, and probably some are using a combination of vehicles.

Save the slash for the special purpose it's supposed to serve. Don't use it when you mean simply *and* or *or*.

As Head of Volunteers/Parents Group Chair at the Maynard School, Gretchen is very busy.

She's Head **and** she's Chair, and she's probably never been so busy in her life. Here's another:

> When you're finished, exit via the front/back door.

You obviously can't do both. An *or* here expresses what the writer meant.

MAKE SURE YOU'VE GOT IT!

Correct the punctuation in the following sentences. You may need to correct more than one error.

1. Sally says do'nt call her out of this meeting, dont' put calls through to her cell phone, and don't let Matt in under any circumstances.
2. The Little Sister Agency serves: the poor and African Americans.
3. Robert Bowers [I wish I'd never heard his name] has asked for your sisters' hand in marriage.
4. Theresa said, "I think we should leave the Robertson's cat out of this".
5. This has been a very-sad meeting, I trust it's decisions will turn out for the best.
6. Gussie Fink-Nottle, an authority on the mating habits of the newt, was hi's friend from grade school days.
7. It's too bad we cannot meet on Thursday, I'm in town for a meeting to discuss some technology at Pratt that's over-the-hill.
8. Jean didn't ask me, however, I'm available if you want me.
9. I loved Charles' well wrapped present: it was a newly-minted $20 gold piece.
10. Please turn to the scene I mentioned, (in Chapter 3) where Joe and Louis meet in the park (p. 40.)
11. Irma asked, "Is your brothers' wife the one who said, "Don't bother" to me on the phone"?
12. Why try to beat up a full grown man.

13. As Alex said, you can hear the chimes from anywhere on-campus. Would you like the on campus tour?

14. Then Sharon-why I did'nt stop her I'll never understand ran straight to the ATM's.

15. I used Alexis' sweater as a pillow on the plane coming home from "Las Vegas."

16. Why didn't you tell me the interest is tax-deductible?

17. Luckily, Freddie has forgotten his laptop, so I wont have to see the photos of his dreadful looking nephews.

18. This photo shows Francis Pinardi, our sales rep, Ginny Maitland, the office manager, Kimberly Sheehan, the senior programmer and me.

19. Our nonEnglish-speaking relatives feel isolated in Wichita.

Answer Key

1. Sally says *don't* call her out of this meeting, *don't* put calls through to her cell phone, and don't let Matt in under any circumstances.

2. The Little Sister Agency *serves* the poor and *African-Americans.*

3. Robert Bowers (I wish I'd never heard his name) has asked for your *sister's* hand in marriage. [NOTE: You could also use dashes instead of parentheses.]

4. Theresa said, "I think we should leave the *Robertsons'* cat out of *this.*"

5. This has been a *very sad* meeting; I trust *its* decisions will turn out for the best.

6. Gussie Fink-Nottle, an authority on the mating habits of the newt, was *his* friend from *grade-school* days.

7. It's too bad we cannot meet on *Thursday.* I'm in town for a meeting to discuss some technology at Pratt that's *over the hill.*

8. Jean didn't ask *me;* however, I'm available if you want me.

9. I loved *Charles's well-wrapped* present: *It* was a *newly minted* $20 gold piece.

10. Please turn to the scene I *mentioned* (in Chapter 3), where Joe and Louis meet in the park (p. *40*).

11. Irma asked, "Is your *brother's* wife the one who said, *'Don't bother'* to me on the *phone?*"

12. Why try to beat up a *full-grown man?*

13. As Alex said, you can hear the chimes from anywhere *on campus.* Would you like the *on-campus* tour?

14. Then Sharon—why I *didn't* stop her I'll never understand—ran straight to the *ATMs.*

15. I used *Alexis's* sweater as a pillow on the plane coming home from *Las Vegas.*

16. Why didn't you tell me the interest is *tax deductible?*

17. Luckily, Freddie has forgotten his laptop, so I *won't* have to see the photos of his *dreadful-looking* nephews.

18. This photo shows Francis Pinardi, our sales rep; Ginny Maitland, the office manager; Kimberly Sheehan, the senior programmer; and me.

19. Our *non-English-speaking* relatives feel isolated in Wichita.

17 Commas: All Things in Moderation

Because there are so many uses for the comma, I'm giving it a chapter of its own.

A friend of mine still remembers the comment a teacher wrote in the margin of her high school composition: "Commas like salt!" My friend had sprinkled commas everywhere throughout the paper because she didn't really know the whys and wherefores of their use. Now a physician, she reads a dark meaning into the remark: Not enough salt is bad for you, and too much can kill you. Pretty accurate: your copy will suffer if you don't have enough commas, but you can really kill it with too many.

I expect you use this handy punctuation mark automatically and correctly most of the time, but enough rules exist so it's hard to know them all. And even if you did learn them all sometime in the past, a little review never hurts. I'm not going to try to include every rule—some of them are even pickier than they ones I *am* including—but rather to highlight some of the ones that reliably trip people up.

Use a Comma Between Complete Sentences Connected by a Conjunction

> Jessica is a lovely girl, but her brains would rattle in a peanut shell.

> I can't live with you, though I care very much for you.

Note that you may not connect sentences joined by a comma and the adverbs *however, moreover, otherwise, therefore,* or *thus,* or (horrors) without **any** connecting word.

No: I saw Michael at the airport, therefore I know he is in town.

No: I asked her to chair the meeting, she said she would be delighted.

These are examples of the infamous run-on sentence, or comma splice, an incorrect as well as an unlovely beast. Sometimes, somewhere, someone occasionally gets away with it—but only with two **very** short and tightly related sentences.

> Don't get mad, get even.

> Bert's wonky, he's a donkey.

You can get away with it if you're an emperor. Julius Caesar got away with a hat trick, in fact:

> I came, I saw, I conquered.

But even the emperor was working with tiny, short sentences. In fact, in his native Latin, each sentence was just one word: *Veni, vidi, vici.* Unless yours are almost that short—just two or three words apiece—don't link them with a comma.

Use Commas in a Series of Names, Words, or Phrases Following All but the LAST Item in the Series

Last is the crucial word in this rule. The serial comma rule says you must put commas after *all items* except the last: for example, the flag is red, white, and blue. Note the comma after *white.* Although somebody publicized a nefarious "rule" some years back saying it was all right to omit the comma after the next-to-last item good grammarians insist for several reasons that you use a comma after that item.

> We were awakened by a huge, hideous, hungry bear.

> George is pleasant, thoughtful, and totally inept.

We need cloth, bandages, and boiling water.

Why insist on that last, or serial, comma? Because otherwise the last two items in the series could be mistaken for a unit and cause ambiguity, if not worse. Here are a few sentences I've craftily confected to prove the point:

> The new t-shirts come in the following colors: red, blue and white, green, pink and purple.

So how many colors do the shirts come in? Is pink and purple one shirt or two? Very ambiguous.

> Susie, Jim and Hannah will be joining us.

Are two people joining us or three? If Susie is being addressed, it's two. If I write "Susie, Jim, and Hannah," there's no confusion.

And then there's the famous (and almost certainly apocryphal) story of the will that left an estate "to be divided in equal parts between my beloved children Tom, Paul and Lily."

We must assume that the lawyer who drafted the will had to leave the country, because Tom supposedly successfully argued that his parent had meant to leave equal parts—*two* parts—one to him, and one to be divided between the luckless Paul and Lily. We must also assume that Lily and Paul failed to send gifts to Tom on his birthday after that. All for the want of a serial comma. Use it. Why chance being misunderstood?

Now here comes an important exception to the rule about commas between words in a series: **Commas are not used between adjectives that describe the entire remainder of a phrase.**

> my old Pancho Gonzales tennis racket

You'd never think to put commas between the adjectives in this case, would you? Occasionally someone does, and it looks ridiculous:

> my, old, Pancho Gonzales, tennis racket

That's because each adjective modifies, or describes, **everything** that comes after it. *Old*, for example, describes *Pancho Gonzales tennis racket*, not just the racket. *Pancho Gonzales* describes *tennis racket*, and so forth.

If that explanation doesn't help, here's another marvelous rule: If you could reasonably reshuffle the adjectives without harming the sentence, then you should put commas between them. For example:

> She is a lovely, intelligent, kind person.

Try it:

> She is a kind, intelligent, lovely person.

Yep. Again:

> She is an intelligent, lovely, kind person.

The sentence works fine with the order of adjectives altered. Each of those adjectives describes *person*, and they can be juggled any way you like. Therefore, it's correct to put commas between them. Let's drag out the old tennis racket and try reordering its adjectives.

> tennis, old, Pancho Gonzales, my, racket

Well, that certainly isn't pretty. I guess those commas aren't such a good idea. Let's try another.

> The Registry is a huge brick building.

Should there be a comma between *huge* and *brick*? If we reverse the order of the two adjectives, we have the following:

> The Registry is a brick, huge building.

It just doesn't work. That's because in the original sentence, *huge* is describing *brick building*, not just *building*. The adjectives aren't on a par with each other, or coordinate.

Otherwise, remember, a comma after every item in a series except the last.

Use Commas to Set Off Nonrestrictive Information

Remember the commas that go around a *which* but not a *that* clause? Nonrestrictive information is material that, similar to the material in a *which* clause, could be omitted from a sentence without damaging the integrity of the sentence—that is, it may be interesting and even important material, but the sentence can stand as a meaningful communication without it.

The old Stuart Circle Hospital, *where I was born*, has been torn down.

Mr. Brown has a terrific coin collection, *including not only a huge American assortment but an impressive European set as well.*

Here is a copy of Casanova's memoirs, *which I think you will like*.

Sometimes the nonrestrictive, or parenthetical, information set off is only a word or two.

He said he was rich, but he is, *in fact*, deeply in debt.

How about bringing some cross-country skis, boots, *etc.*, for our trek?

The sentence is structurally sound without the information, which adds a fact, sometimes what you could call "by-the-way" information. We show that relationship by hooking commas around such material.

Use Comma Pairs to Set Off Appositives if the Information Is Nonrestrictive

An appositive is a noun that repeats, clarifies, or identifies the noun that precedes it.

My brother Mark is an investor who collects paintings.

Sheila, *my partner in Hughes Design*, is a CPA.

Former hockey great Bobby Orr is still adored by fans.

Mark, my partner in Hughes Designs, and *Bobby Orr* are the appositives in the preceding examples. Each adds information about the preceding noun or noun form.

As you might guess by the commas or lack of commas in these examples, an appositive can be either restrictive or non-restrictive. In the first example, *Mark* is restrictive: The name identifies him as one of several brothers. If I have only one brother, the correct form would be:

My brother, Mark, is an investor who collects paintings.

In the second example, *my partner in Hughes Designs*, is non-restrictive: It adds a fact about Sheila, but she's already been iden-tified. And in the third example the information is restrictive: *Bobby Orr* tells *which* former hockey great.

These appositives work the same way that the restrictive/nonrestrictive clauses we examined previously do, so don't let them intimidate you.

Put Commas in Pairs Around Clauses and Words

Use a pair of commas rather than using just one comma, unless the clause is at the very beginning or end of your sentence. Don't forget that second comma. Even those tiny Latin abbreviations, such as *etc.*, *e.g.*, and *i.e.*, always have **two** commas bracketing them.

No: Ernest Shackleton's ill-fated trip to Antarctica, undertaken in 1915 is a story of incredible heroism and endurance.

Yes: Ernest Shackleton's ill-fated trip to Antarctica, undertaken in 1915, is a story of incredible heroism and endurance.

No: My watch, which keeps perfect time says it is 9:25.

Yes: My watch, which keeps perfect time, says it is 9:25.

Use a Comma to Prevent a Misreading

Having proposed an assessment for the new kitchen and investigating another for a hydraulic hoist, Ben voted against a dues increase.

A casual reader could perceive *kitchen* and *investigating* as two items to be paid for by assessment. In such a case, a comma clarifies the issue.

Having proposed an assessment for the new kitchen, and investigating another for a hydraulic hoist, Ben voted against a dues increase.

Here's another:

Sylvia told Joan she smelled gas and called Muni Gas and Light.

This sentence could either mean that Silvia told Joan she smelled gas and also told her she had called the gas company, or that she

> **Just for Fun**
> Can you punctuate and add capital letters so this sentence makes sense?
>
> That that is is that that is not is not is not that it it is
>
> Answer: That that is, is; that that is not, is not. Is not that it? It is.

made her announcement to Joan and *then* proceeded to call the company. If you put a comma after gas, it's clearly the latter.

Don't get all crazy with this rule and start littering your copy with commas: Employ a comma only if a comma's needed to prevent a misunderstanding.

When a Clause or Phrase Begins a Sentence, Place a Comma at the End of the Clause

You know the type of sentence. An introductory clause comes *before* the verb and subject that are the meat of the sentence. For example:

> *After spending a wonderful afternoon on the boat*, Emily and Dan had dinner at The Daily Catch on the fish pier.

> *Although we don't meet often*, Jack is my favorite uncle.

> *To answer your last question*, zero to the power of 10 is still zero.

Note: When an infinitive such as "to answer..." here *is the subject* of a sentence, do not use a comma after it.

> *To train for a marathon* takes many hours of training and serious dedication.

There's an old rule that you may omit the comma after an introductory phrase that is fewer than five words long.

> In 1917 the Revolution crippled Russia's war effort.

> When in Rome do as the Romans do.

The rule doesn't hold in all cases, however:

> As expected, he failed to appear at the spa.

Let your ear guide you on these clauses: If you pause at the end, a comma is probably indicated. Don't take this as a mandate to insert a comma every time you breathe! There's too much of that around already. Commas like salt.

Use Commas Around Interjections

> *Ah*, the joy of getting up late and having the whole day to play!

> Then I think, *oh*, to be 16 again!

Use Commas to Set Off the Name of Someone Being Addressed

Carrie said, "Tell me, Grace, have you thought of acting in films?"

Hey, Jason, where are you going with that chainsaw?

Use Commas to Set Off Absolute Phrases. Absolute Phrases Are Clauses Featuring a Subject and a Participle, or *-ing* Verb Form

The deed having been done, Robin Hood rode off in search of the sheriff.

We knew we had little time to work, *the sun setting promptly at 4:00.*

The lecture was a bore, *the speaker knowing little about his subject*, and Elaine promptly fell asleep.

Use a Comma Ahead of a Direct Quotation

Kate said, "You promised to be here before the play started."

Use a Comma to Separate Contradictory Parts of a Sentence

I am a lover, not a fighter.

I am not a fighter, but a lover.

Use a Comma Between Repeated Words to Prevent Confusion

What the real meaning of the act is, is not entirely clear.

We then set to, to strike the tents and break camp.

Both of those examples are ugly, too. You may be better off doing a rewrite when you see twin words looming.

The real meaning of the act is not entirely clear.

We hurried to strike the tents and break camp.

Use Commas to Set Off Elements of Place, Addresses, and Dates

The family lived at 111 Renwick Drive, Ithaca, New York.

The hit reality show actually originated in Rome, Georgia.

On November 11, 1918, the guns fell silent at last.

Note that no comma is used between a state name or abbreviation and a zip code, either in an address or in running copy.

My address is 10 McLean Avenue, Richmond, VA 23221.

45 Flint St.
Philadelphia, PA 19090

Please observe that these commas come in pairs! There will be no pity shown to anyone who writes the following:

February 23, 1988 was his birthday.

No comma is used with a date that does not include the day of the month:

June 1944

November 2009

Finally, please note that all commas, regardless of logic, go **inside** quotation marks.

Did she say, "I don't love him," and slam the door?

His final line, "Threaten the head that I love," is deeply moving.

Same goes for periods. Now take 20 seconds to complain that it doesn't make sense and you're sure you've seen it the other way round. You may well have done so: In any book printed in the UK, for example, you'll find commas and periods inside or outside quotation marks, depending on whether the mark is part of the quoted material or not. But in the United States, this is the rule.

A story, which may be simply a myth told to explain this aberration on our side of the pond, says that in days long ago when all type had to be set by hand, printers (at least American printers: The Brits were made of sterner stuff—look at the Battle of Britain) were distressed and annoyed that the tiny little marks, the commas and the periods, kept falling off the line of type. Quotation marks, by contrast, stayed put. Maybe because they sit higher up, the piece of type was bigger. At any rate, the printers found that if the tiny marks were enclosed within the second quotation mark, the whole shebang stayed on the line. They began therefore to put the quotation mark protectively *after* the commas and periods, sense or nonsense, and it's been that way ever since. Well. At least it may help you remember.

Some dictionaries give exhaustive (and exhausting—you thought this was bad) explanations of comma function, in the unlikely event you want more. *Words into Type* has an amazing section on the comma as well as other marks of punctuation.

✳ IN BRIEF

▷ Use a comma between two complete sentences connected by a conjunction.

▷ Use commas in a series of names, words, or phrases following all but the LAST item in the series.

▷ Use commas to set off nonrestrictive information.

▷ Use comma pairs to set off appositives if the information is nonrestrictive.

▷ Put commas in pairs around clauses and words.

▷ Use a comma to prevent a misreading.

▷ When a clause or phrase begins a sentence, place a comma at the end of the clause.

▷ Use commas around interjections.

▷ Use commas to set off the name of someone being addressed.

▷ Use commas to set off absolute phrases.

▷ Use a comma preceding a direct quotation.

▷ Use a comma to separate two contradictory parts of a sentence.

▷ Use a comma between repeated words to prevent confusion.

▷ Use commas to set off elements of place, addresses, and dates.

MAKE SURE YOU'VE GOT IT!

Add or delete commas if necessary to make the following sentences correct.

1. Laura was my mentor, and my idol as well.

2. Professor Fagles translated *The Iliad*, *The Odyssey* and *The Aeneid* before his death, in March, 2008.

3. While you were daydreaming by the creek Davy finished all the chores.

4. It was not really a coat but a heavy shirt.

5. Hi Babe—oh are you still angry with me, for putting eggs in your bed?

6. Jeff offered me his purple scarf which was perfect with my outfit.

7. To err, is human.

8. An inexperienced, poorly rehearsed firing squad shot Tosca by mistake.

9. What it was was baseball.

10. Stanley said "I had no idea she was so talented", which astonished me.

11. The Pinot Noir scene being over I was ready to leave.

Answer Key

1. Laura was my *mentor and* my idol as well.

2. Professor Fagles translated *The Iliad*, *The Odyssey*, and *The Aeneid* before his *death* in *March 2008*.

3. While you were daydreaming by the *creek,* Davy finished all the chores.

4. It was not really a *coat,* but a heavy shirt.

5. *Hi,* Babe—*oh,* are you still angry with *me* for putting eggs in your bed?

6. Jeff offered me his purple *scarf,* which was perfect with my outfit.

7. To *err is* human.

8. An inexperienced, poorly rehearsed firing squad shot Tosca by mistake. CORRECT AS WRITTEN

9. What it *was,* was baseball.

10. Stanley *said*, "I had no idea she was so *talented*," which astonished me.

11. The Pinot Noir scene being *over*, I was ready to leave.

Capital Letters:
Where, When, Why

Probably the most important thing to remember about capitalizing is that, if you think you shouldn't, you're probably right. The Germans use initial capitals on all their nouns, and some other things also; they're used to it, but we're not, and it doesn't take too many caps before your work looks funny. The overuse of capital letters makes the line of your prose ragged: Your sentence stutters up and down, making it harder to read. You may look outdated and hokey. You may also come off sounding like a cross between Winnie the Pooh and Hitler. Achtung! Ich bin ein Führer of Very Little Brain.

I hope I'm frightening you. The fewer caps you get away with, the better I look.

The Victorians were cap artists: 19th-century English novels abound with initial caps, as do American works of the same era. The Brits still throw caps around more freely than we do. But for the past century or so, the trend in English has been away from initial capitals, and today the style in the United States is definitely "down cap," so leave them out if you have a choice. This is not to say that the choice is always yours. You may work for an organization that has its own set of rules for capitalizing. If you do, follow them. And there are some places where just about everyone agrees capital letters are appropriate.

In fact, there are quite a few. It's not uncommon to see 30 pages in some manuals on when to use or not use capital letters. I'm not planning to do that to you, but here are a few important highlights.

Capitalize Proper Names of People, Including Familiar Nicknames, the Pronoun I, and the Titles of Relatives if Used as Names

my friends and I   Aunt Suzanne   Old Hickory   Prince Charles

Do **not** capitalize the titles of relatives when they aren't part of a proper name, as Aunt Suzanne is in the previous example.

No: I haven't seen my Mother for fifteen years.

Yes: Jerry Garcia began his career with Mother McCree's Uptown Jug Champions.

No: My friend says it's okay to marry your First Cousin if you both have a lot of good genes.

Yes: Oh, no! Father has invited Cousin Bobby and Fat Aunt Sadie Who Never Smiles for the holidays!

Capitalize Titles if They Come Before a Name; After a Name, Lowercase

Mayor Brown	Tom Brown, mayor of Springfield
Pope Benedict	Does Benedict, the pope, wear a dress?
Inspector Clouseau	a visit from the inspector

No: We're having dinner with Stephen Millan, Vice President of AgVen.

Yes: We're having dinner with AgVen Vice President Stephen Millan.

Yes: We're having dinner with Stephen Millan, vice president of AgVen.

Capitalize the Names of Businesses and Divisions of Businesses, Groups, Organizations, and Teams

Apple Computer	the Minnesota Vikings
the Hardy Mums	Greenpeace
the Republican Party	Mortgage Loan Division
International Business Machines	P&G Research & Development

Capitalize Registered or Trademarked Names

Kleenex	Dumpster	Realtor
Coca Cola	Band-Aid	Visa

✳ 173

By the way, these companies would also very much like for you to use the ® or ™ symbol with their names, at least once on a page or in a piece. I don't know why they bother; doesn't everybody say kleenex and band-aids? I know we should be saying tissues and bandages, but that horse left the barn a long time ago.

Capitalize the Names of Divisions of Government and Legislative Bodies

Houses of Parliament   Senate

Game and Fisheries Division   Federal Trade Commission

Registry of Motor Vehicles   the Oregon State Legislature

But brace yourself: **Don't** capitalize *federal government*, *U.S. government*, or *state government*. These are considered generic, as opposed to the Federal Trade Commission or the Oregon State Legislature, which are proper names.

Capitalize All Letters in Acronyms

IBM   ATM   BS, MA

NASCAR   MADD   PC

Write People's Personal Titles With Upper- and Lowercase Letters

Dr.   Mr.   Ms.   Jr.   Esq.

Capitalize Proper Nouns Referring to Geographic Regions and Locations, Including Popular Terms of Reference for Them

New York   the Northeast

the East Coast   the South Pole

the Middle East   the Dust Bowl

the Empire State   the United Kingdom

Do NOT Capitalize Simple Directions

Atlantic City is southeast of Philadelphia.

Go west on Interstate 90 until you come to the outskirts of Seattle.

Capitalize the Names of Mountains and Bodies of Water

Lake Ontario	Indian Ocean	Mount Everest
Loch Ness	Tappahannock River	Goose Creek
the Atlantic	the Alps	the Panama Canal

Capitalize the Names of Languages, Ethnicities, and Religious and Political Groups

Serbo-Croatian	Christian Scientists
Asian-American	Sephardic Jews
French	Democrats
Iroquois	Hinduism

Capitalize the Names of Scientific, Philosophic, and Cultural Movements

Freudianism	Transcendentalism	Darwinism	Stoicism

Do NOT Capitalize Fields of Study

economics	molecular biology	mathematics	geology

Study of a language or history of a country is of course an exception.

majoring in French	Spanish
American history	English literature

Capitalize Adjectives Created out of Proper Names

Bermuda shorts	Pilgrim settlements	Dutch Elm disease
California roll	Bernese mountain dog	Swedish immigrants

BUT check your dictionary before you capitalize the adjectives attached to familiar items. Many places have contributed their names to foods and other familiar things. Some have become so much a part of our English language that they are no longer capitalized. For example:

french fries	cashmere sweater	oxford cloth shirt
russian dressing	roman and italic type	madras pants

For Medical Terms, Capitalize Adjectives Created Out of Proper Names if They Are Possessives

Baker's cyst	Huntington's chorea
Alzheimer's disease	Legionnaire's disease

Note that many medical adjectives derived from proper names but not possessives are not capitalized.

caesarian birth

fallopian tubes

parkinsonian syndrome (a set of symptoms resembling Parkinson's disease)

NOTE: The words for illnesses, conditions, diseases, parts of the body, and medical events are not themselves capitalized.

Hodgkin's *disease*
Achilles' *tendon*
Reye's *syndrome*
Babinski *reflex*

Capitalize the Names of Every Religion's God(s), Goddess(es), Lesser Deities, Prophets, and Sacred Texts, Whether Current or Historical

Allah	God, the Lord	Jesus Christ
Jehovah	the Bible	Mohammed
the Koran	the Book of Mormon	Baal
Osiris	the Virgin Mary	the Upanishads

Note that the titles Bible and Koran, the books within them (Genesis, Exodus, and so forth), and the titles of some other texts sacred to their religions are not italicized.

Capitalize Days of the Week, Months, Historical Periods, and Holidays

Monday	the Christian Era	the Renaissance
July	Martin Luther King Day	the Fourth of July

Do NOT Capitalize Seasons of the Year

spring	summer	fall, autumn	winter

Do NOT Capitalize Centuries, Whether Nouns or Adjectives

the fifth century BC   eighth-century tapestry

Capitalize Important Events and Some Famous *Things*

Earth Day	the Cold War
the Johnstown Flood	the Children's Crusade
the Cuban Missile Crisis	the Blizzard of '78

I do realize a lot of this is truly arbitrary, but if it made perfect sense I wouldn't need to write it down for you. Because it's irrational, everyone has to read up at least some of the time.

Capitalize the Word That Begins a Sentence

You knew that. But there's an exception: Inside parentheses, a sentence does *not* need to be capitalized.

> She was hired as his companion (he was newly blind and learning how to cope) but became a dear friend as well.

> They went for a walk (through the woods. He didn't want her going alone) after dinner.

To me, that second example looks odd, but obviously *He* needs to be capitalized. I'd probably rewrite the sentence.

Capitalize the Word that Begins a Direct Quotation

Celia answered, "We asked her not to mention the will to Dolores."

Use a Capital Letter After a Colon if the Following Material Is a Complete Sentence

He was convinced of it: She had lied to him repeatedly.

Let's travel light: We'll be gone just three days.

But: He talked about what he knew best: the Russian Revolution.

Capitalize the Titles of Books, Speeches, Poems, Newspapers, Magazines, Movies, Songs, and Plays and Their Parts (Scenes, Articles, Chapters) Using Headline Style

Have you read Ken Follett's latest book, *World Without End?*

His lecture was entitled "Why Global Warming Isn't Our Fault."

Headline style means capping the important words: usually the nouns, pronouns, adjectives, adverbs, and verbs. That means, and this may be an easier way to look at it, *not* to capitalize prepositions (*in, under, to, around, with*), articles (*a, an, the*), or conjunctions (*and, but, or*). Some authorities, with whom I agree, cap extra-long prepositions, such as *without* in Ken Follett's book title in the preceding example. Also, the first and last words of your headline, title, or whatever should be capitalized.

> Also note that some publishers (including Career Press, the publisher of this book) use numerals for all numbers and ordinals in heading and headlines.

Headless Body Found in Topless Bar

Love in an Elevator

As Time Goes By

Many organizations now capitalize if a word is longer than four or five letters. Be sure you know house style if you are writing for an organization or business.

Also, note that you are not supposed to lowercase all little words! Though that's often what's happening, because prepositions, articles, and conjunctions tend to be little. The verb forms *is*, *be*, and *has*, for example, need to be capitalized despite their size.

Love Is Blue

How Many Children Had Lady Macbeth?

Moreover, many publications ask that you initial cap both parts of a verb, such as *made up*, even if the second word is just a couple of letters.

> Jury Agrees Defendant Made Up Story of Armed Intruder

Capitalize Both Halves of a Hyphenated Compound Unless It Is a Permanent Compound

> The Art of 20th-Century Japanese Printmakers
>
> Cost-Conscious Teens Turn to Thrift Shops

In general, don't capitalize the second half of permanent compounds (those that are always hyphenated).

> Coexisting with Your Mother-in-law
>
> Virginians Re-create Battle of Bull Run

Note that the former is not a universal rule. Some organizations disagree and *do* initial cap the second part.

Check your dictionary: If it's there with a hyphen, it's always hyphenated. If your organization has a rule regarding the capitals, follow it. Otherwise, stick with me and be consistent.

Although I mentioned that less is more when it comes to capitalizing, I have to make an exception for you marketing types. The advertising industry is sorely in need of ways to attract attention, and capital letters are among the easiest tools for doing so in print:

> Gigantic, Colossal Presidents' Day Sale! Prices Slashed!
> Hurry in TODAY!

So maybe that's a little over the top, but you get the idea. Here's a more restrained effort:

> Private Showing for Museum Members Only:
> *Farinelli*
> A Film about the Most Famous Castrato of His or Any Time

※ IN BRIEF

≫ Capitalize proper names of people, including familiar nicknames, the pronoun I, and the titles of relatives if used as names.

> Capitalize titles if they come before a name; after a name, lowercase.
> Capitalize the names of businesses and divisions of businesses, groups, organizations, and teams.
> Capitalize registered or trademarked names.
> Capitalize the names of divisions of government and legislative bodies.
> Capitalize all letters in acronyms.
> Write people's personal titles with upper- and lowercase letters.
> Capitalize proper nouns referring to geographic regions and locations, including popular terms of reference for them.
> Do NOT capitalize simple directions.
> Capitalize the names of mountains and bodies of water.
> Capitalize the names of languages, ethnicities, and religious and political groups.
> Capitalize the names of scientific, philosophic, and cultural movements.
> Do NOT capitalize fields of study.
> Capitalize adjectives created out of proper names.
> For medical terms, capitalize adjectives created out of a proper name if they are possessives.
> Capitalize the names of every religion's god(s), goddess(es), lesser deities, prophets, and sacred texts, whether current or historical.
> Capitalize days of the week, months, historical periods, and holidays.
> Do NOT capitalize seasons of the year.
> Do NOT capitalize centuries, whether nouns or adjectives.
> Capitalize important events and some famous *things*.
> Capitalize the first word in a sentence.

> Capitalize the first word of a direct quotation.

> Use a capital letter after a colon if the following material is a complete sentence.

> Capitalize the titles of books, speeches, poems, newspapers, magazines, movies, songs, and plays and their parts (scenes, articles, chapters) using headline style.

> Capitalize both halves of a hyphenated compound unless it is a permanent compound.

MAKE SURE YOU'VE GOT IT!

Correct the capital and lowercase letters as necessary:

1. He has a BA degree in English Literature, but his real love is Botany.
2. We drove over the Golden gate bridge at sunset.
3. Headline: Dead Woman was Friend To All, Say Horrified Neighbors
4. I think I'll just have a hamburger and French fries.
5. The 1906 San Francisco earthquake resulted in 3,000 deaths.
6. Headline: Ringo has New Sticks to Beat the Drum with
7. He's an entertaining fellow if you're into the black death in 14th-Century Europe.
8. If I had any training in Physiology I could tell you what your Resting Heart Rate means.
9. The lecture is entitled "The Half-Brother of Genghis Khan."
10. The great Tenor Walter Slezak looked at his watch and asked, "when does the next swan leave?"
11. Julia says the U.S. Government is to blame for her bad plastic surgery results and wants to take her case to the supreme court.
12. Next Winter I plan to write a Gothic Romance during our break.

13. A Lancet Study shows premature babies are at a higher risk for Autism.
14. Here's an idea: One nut from each of the other wheels to secure the fourth tire.
15. I believe Hansen's Disease is another name for Leprosy.

Answer Key

1. He has a BA degree in English *literature,* but his real love is *botany.*
2. We drove over the *Golden Gate Bridge* at sunset.
3. Headline: Dead Woman *Was* Friend *to* All, Say Horrified Neighbors
4. I think I'll just have a hamburger and *french fries.*
5. The 1906 *San Francisco Earthquake* resulted in 3,000 deaths.
6. Headline: Ringo *Has* New Sticks to Beat the Drum *With*
7. He's an entertaining fellow if you're into the *Black Death* in *fourteenth-century* Europe.
8. If I had any training in *physiology* I could tell you what your *resting heart rate* means.
9. The lecture is entitled "The *Half-brother* of Genghis Khan." OR CORRECT AS WRITTEN
10. The great *tenor* Walter Slezak looked at his watch and asked, "*When* does the next swan leave?"
11. Julia says the U.S. *government* is to blame for her bad plastic surgery results and wants to take her case to the *Supreme Court.*
12. Next *winter* I plan to write a *gothic romance* during our break.
13. A Lancet *study* shows premature babies are at a higher risk for *autism.*
14. Here's an idea: *one* nut from each of the other wheels to secure the fourth tire.
15. I believe *Hansen's disease* is another name for *leprosy.*

Abbreviations: The Short of It

We've touched on abbreviations and acronyms in various parts of this book, but here's everything that I think is worth saying about them. As you have probably noticed, when you read newspapers, magazines, and mail, there's some variation in the way abbreviations are handled. There are several correct ways to do so. If you are writing for a business or organization, follow its house style by all means. If that's not the case, this chapter is for you. Remember that consistency is important: Don't write *B.A.* with periods and *MA* without them.

First, let's define our terms. An **abbreviation** is a shortened form of a word or words.

Dr. for doctor or Drive	*BA* for Bachelor of Arts degree
Ave. for Avenue	*no.* for number

A **contraction** is a type of abbreviation in which usually part of the middle is omitted.

int'l for international	*can't* for cannot	*am't* for amount
ass'n for association	*sec'y* for secretary	*shouldn't* for should not

Note: Don't put a period after a contraction.

An **acronym** is another type of abbreviation, usually composed of the first letters of a name, title, or thing.

BLT for a bacon, lettuce, and tomato sandwich

Sometimes an acronym combines initial and non-initial letters.

radar comes from RAdio Detection And Ranging

Americans love acronyms. They come to us from industry/technology (*GPS* for global positioning system), from business

(*FYI* for, for your information), from medicine (*AMA* for the American Medical Association; *AIDS* for acquired immune deficiency [or immunodeficiency] syndrome), and from the Internet (*ROFL* for rolling on the floor laughing).

Many acronyms are pronounceable (*CAD/CAM* for computer-aided design/computer-aided manufacturing; *NATO* for the North Atlantic Treaty Organization). Others (such as *FBI* and *RV*) are not pronounceable. Still others are pronounceable, but we don't pronounce them (*USA, CIA, UCLA*). They're all acronyms, according to the dictionary definition.

Here are some guidelines for handling abbreviations.

The Tendency Today Is to Write Abbreviations Without Periods

I'm not out on a limb here: This has been happening for some time. Many organizations no longer use periods in the abbreviations of their names. Colleges are writing BA instead of B.A., banks write ATM and EFT, and acronyms almost never sport periods. In fact, most abbreviations totally in uppercase letters do without periods, whereas those with lowercase or a mix of upper- and lowercase letters generally have them.

Yes: Bettina is getting her Ph.D. in economics.

Yes: I have asked Maj. Gen. Buzz Hirschorn to join us.

Do Use Periods in Certain Situations

❋ Use a period with most abbreviations associated with people's names.

| Mrs. | Dr. | Jr. | Esq. | Ph.D. |

❋ Use a period with people's initials.

| B.B. King | J.D. Salinger | J.J. Abrams |

❋ Use a period with Latin abbreviations, those lowercased little words.

| *etc.* | and so forth | *i.e.* | that is |
| *e.g.* | for example | *ca.* | around, approximately |

✳ Use a period with the time-of-day abbreviations a.m. and p.m.

    9:00 p.m.   11:15 a.m.

Don't put a space after the internal periods in any of these abbreviations.

When an Abbreviation at the End of a Sentence Ends in a Period, Don't Add Another Period

No: He promised to meet us at the Empire State Building at 1:00 p.m..

Yes: He promised to meet us at the Empire State Building at 1:00 p.m.

Don't Put an Apostrophe Following Most Abbreviations to Create a Plural

In fact, please don't: It's confusing. This is an old-fashioned effort to be clear, which unfortunately, to our twenty-first-century eyes, looks like a possessive form. In most cases, you can simply add an *s*.

No: YMCA's

Yes: YMCAs

No: DVD's

Yes: DVDs

Don't Capitalize Words Just Because Their Abbreviation Is in Caps

        ATM *but* automated teller machine

        SUV *but* sport utility vehicle

Use *A* or *An* Depending on How You Pronounce an Abbreviation

Many people have trouble with which article to use before an abbreviation. (Sometimes even on billboards—how humiliating is that?) Is it *a* MBA degree, like *a* magazine, because *m* is a consonant? Is it *a* FBI agent? Is it *an* NATO agreement? No, it's not, and there's a rule: The article and abbreviation must pass the read-aloud test. Because the *m* and *f* in the first two examples are pronounced *em* and *eff*, the correct choice is *an*. In the last, NATO is pronounced as a word, so the correct article is *a*.   ✳ 185

No: She asked whether Tim had received *a MBA* degree.

Yes: She asked whether Tim had received *an MBA* degree.

No: The next morning, *a FBI* agent was at my door.

Yes: The next morning, *an FBI* agent was at my door.

The same holds true for any abbreviation or acronym pronounced with a beginning vowel sound.

No: The president was told that *a* SST was being developed.

Yes: The president was told that *an* SST was being developed..

No: Susan's in the country, complete with *a RFD* address!

Yes: Susan's in the country, complete with *an RFD* address!

For acronyms pronounced like words, you also use *a* or *an* depending on whether they begin with a vowel or a consonant sound.

No: The secretary general brokered *an NATO* agreement.

Yes: The secretary general brokered *a NATO* agreement.

No: James is *an U.S.* citizen because he was born in Topeka.

Yes: James is *a U.S.* citizen because he was born in Topeka.

An Abbreviation Should Not Begin a Sentence

Like starting a sentence with a number, it just looks odd. Titles (for example, Mr. and Dr.) are exceptions.

No: No. 6 is being actively recruited for the major leagues.

Yes: Scouts for the major leagues are actively recruiting No. 6.

When Using an Abbreviation That May Be Unfamiliar to Readers, Write Out the Whole Name or Title, Then Give the Abbreviation in Parentheses

Then use the abbreviation freely without further identification.

The *National Collegiate Athletic Association (NCAA)* women's gymnastics championship is dominated by Georgia.

Here are a few more teeny, tiny, important rules to observe:

✸ Although *US* (or *U.S.*) as an adjective is fine, good style frowns on *US* or *U.S.* as a noun except in very informal writing. Spell it out: *United States.*

✸ Don't abbreviate *versus* in running copy. If you're writing footnotes, *vs.* is all right.

✸ Remember that in lawsuits *versus* is abbreviated *v.*

✸ The plural of *St.* as an abbreviation for *Saint* is *SS*: *SS Peter, James, and John.*

✸ Finally, and importantly, don't hesitate to use the abbreviations noted in this section and others like them, taking care to identify acronyms that may be unfamiliar to your readers. Stay away from symbols (<, >, &, #, %,°) and technical abbreviations, however, unless you are writing scientific or technical material.

✸ IN BRIEF

≫ The tendency today is to write abbreviations without periods.

≫ Do use periods in certain situations.

≫ When an abbreviation at the end of a sentence ends in a period, don't add a second period.

≫ Don't put an apostrophe following most abbreviations to create a plural.

≫ Don't capitalize words just because their abbreviation is in caps.

≫ Use *a* or *an* depending on how you pronounce an abbreviation.

≫ An abbreviation should not begin a sentence.

≫ When using an abbreviation that may be unfamiliar to readers, write out the whole name or title first, then give the abbreviation in parentheses.

✷ 187

MAKE SURE YOU'VE GOT IT!

Correct the abbreviations in the following sentences as necessary.

1. Sincerely, Charles Dixon, Ass't. Director
2. Gordon brought me an UCLA sweatshirt from his trip.
3. She founded FIB (Falsehoods in Business) to help combat unethical behavior.
4. I slept in YMCA's all the way across the US.
5. I begged her not to get into an NASCAR race with no training.
6. Dr. Walcott is a medical doctor, not a Ph.D..
7. BA degrees are just the first step toward a good job nowadays.
8. It's the 21st century, and you can't play Compact Disks (CDs) on a Video Cassette Recorder (VCR).
9. His best friend is a FBI agent—tight-lipped, cool, intrepid, etc..
10. J. D. Salinger rarely appears in public.

Answer Key

1. Sincerely, Charles Dixon, *Ass't* Director
2. Gordon brought me *a* UCLA sweatshirt from his trip.
3. She founded *Falsehoods in Business (FIB)* to help combat unethical behavior.
4. I slept in *YMCAs* all the way across the *United States*.
5. I begged her not to get into *a* NASCAR race with no training.
6. Dr. Walcott is a medical doctor, not a *Ph.D.*
7. *A* BA degree is just the first step toward a good job nowadays.
8. It's the 21st century, and you can't play *compact disks* (CDs) on a *video cassette recorder* (VCR).
9. His best friend is *an* FBI agent—tight-lipped, cool, intrepid, *etc.*
10. *J.D.* Salinger rarely appears in public. THERE SHOULD NOT BE A SPACE BETWEEN "J." AND "D."

Numbers:
Rules of the Game

Many rules exist for the treatment of numbers, and, depending on the kind of writing you do (and the organization you represent, if you're writing for an organization), certain conventions may apply or not. Here is an overview of some generally accepted rules.

Write Numbers Below 10 as Words; Use Numerals for 10 and Greater

This convention, or some version of it, is widely accepted. *The Chicago Manual of Style* requires that you write out numbers through 99. Some organizations write them out through 20. Choose the form that works for you.

> Let's invite *six* for bridge at each table and hope that *four* or *five* will be able to come.

> You should include *25* stems in each bouquet.

The same rule applies to the ordinals—those are the *–st*, *–nd*, *–rd*, and *–th* words.

> This is the *third* time I have reminded you about dinner on the *24th*.

If you don't like this rule, make up your own. (Don't make a habit of doing this.) It's perfectly okay to write out one through ten, or one through a hundred, or whatever you like, as long as you are consistent.

Exceptions to the Numbers Rule Abound

Note that there's quite a crew of exceptions to the rule. And sometimes the exceptions have exceptions…. Here they come.

Dates

September 8, 2009   Expiration Date: 01/31/10   the '60s, the 1970s

However, you should spell out (and lowercase) centuries: *the eighteenth century.*

Time of Day

6:00 a.m.   3:15 p.m.   12 noon   12 midnight

Note that a.m. and p.m. are written with lowercase letters and followed by periods with no spaces between.

By the way, some people write *12:00 a.m.* for midnight and *12:00 p.m.* for noon; other people object, because *a.m.* means before the meridian and *p.m.* means after the meridian. (*Meridian* is from the Latin word for noon.) They think you should write *12m* for both, so everybody can be mixed up. Personally I think *12 a.m.* sounds like daytime and *12 p.m.* sounds like nighttime, which isn't the case, so I like *12 noon* and *12 midnight.*

Some people (those folks again!) think *12 noon* and *12 midnight* are redundant: if it's midnight, it's 12, right? Maybe it does sound a little hokey (like saying *Paris, France*), but I think if you write simply *noon*, it could mean around the noon hour, as opposed to exactly at 12. A word to the wise.

Do not ever write *9:00 a.m. in the morning* or *10:00 p.m. at night*. Talk about hokey.

Street Addresses

79 Rice Road
Richmond, VT 98190

1179 24th Street, NW
Omaha, WA 02458

But spell out numerical street names under 10.

Fifth Avenue

Decimals and Percentages

12.09   .0001   0.68   7 percent   100 percent

Note: In scientific or technical material, you may use the % sign, always with figures.

Numbered Parts of a Book or Other Document

Chapter 8   Section IV   Act 3, part 44, line 8

Size and Dimension

4 feet square   a perfect size 6

There's wiggle room here. You may prefer to express dimensions in words, depending on the type of writing you're doing:

Charlie stood a full six feet five inches tall.

With Abbreviations and Symbols

25 mg   No. 11   8° N   < 4

Temperature

72 degrees   36° F (use symbol for sci/tech writing)

Recipes

3 T butter

Amounts of Money

$2.50 $526,244.63 $400 in small bills $.35

If I were writing a novel, I might use words for small amounts: *He begged for five dollars to take the subway home.* Note that *35 cents* is also fine if you're not writing a series of amounts of money.

It's not generally necessary to place zeroes after whole dollar amounts: $25. If you're writing legal or financial documents, of course, that's a different matter: You should include the two zeroes after whole amounts to be absolutely clear. Also, in a series of mixed numbers, it's customary to include the zeroes to show that no pennies were accidentally omitted.

$45.26, $14.72, $62.*00*,

Votes

By 5 votes to 1, we voted to disband.

Scores

The Bruins won 7-3.   Orioles 8, Yankees 4

If You Have a Mixture of Numbers Greater Than and Less Than 10 Referring to Similar Things, Express Them as Either All Numerals or All Words

Fearing her family was animal impaired, she bought them a small farm: *12 horses, 4 cows, 10 sheep*, and a miniature donkey.

We're available to help *24* hours a day, *7* days a week.

When 2 Numbers Are Side by Side, Alternate Between Numerals and Words

No: I'll need *36 .5-inch* bolts for the bookcase.

Yes: I'll need *thirty-six .5-inch* bolts for the bookcase.

Yes: I'll need *36 half-inch* bolts for the bookcase.

No: She had *10 100s* sewn into her hem, which struck me as suspicious.

Yes: She had *10 hundreds* sewn into her hem, which struck me as suspicious.

Yes: She had *ten 100s* sewn into her hem, which struck me as suspicious.

Write Out Rounded-Off or Approximate Numbers

I believe there are around *thirty thousand* students enrolled.

It looked as if *two hundred* or so boats were moored in the tiny harbor.

Rounded Numbers Greater Than a Million Are Written as a Numeral Plus a Word

It's estimated people have been on earth for *5 million years* or more.

Geological data on the Arctic Ocean indicate *400 billion* barrels of oil may lie beneath it.

Write Out a Number at the Beginning of a Sentence

If you don't like the way it looks, you can usually rewrite so the number appears elsewhere.

> *Seventeen* of the fourth-graders were never seen again.

> *Nineteen forty-five* is the year I was born and the war ended.

I'd probably rewrite that second one this way:

> I was born in 1945, the year the war ended.

Write Out People's Ages Except in Scientific or Technical Copy

> Danae was *forty-two* years old, but she could easily pass for *thirty-two*.

> Henry was a very energetic *four-year-old*.

> Patient is a pleasant *72-year-old* man with COPD and peripheral neuropathy.

> A sample of women *aged 25 to 75* reveals significant changes in bone density.

Numbers 21 through 99 Are Hyphenated When Written Out; Larger Numbers Are Not Hyphenated

> *Thirty-two* teeth is standard issue, but most adults do not have a full set.

> Maisie received more than *two hundred* get-well cards.

> *Three thousand one hundred seventy-five* certainly is a lot of bees.

The ordinals (twenty-third, fifty-sixth, and so on) work the same way.

> She was approximately the *one hundred fifty-fifth* baby to be named Victoria Japonica in 1945.

Don't Use Ordinal Numbers When Writing Dates if the Month Comes Before the Day

Some people have trouble remembering this because when you pronounce *May 5*, for example, you actually pronounce the *th*: "May 5th." But that's the rule.

No: *February 23rd* is Clarissa's 40th birthday, and when she wakes up there will be 40 flamingos on her lawn.

Yes: *February 23* is Clarissa's 40th birthday, and when she wakes up there will be 40 flamingos on her lawn.

No: My stepchildren will be visiting *July 21st* through *July 25th.*

Yes: My stepchildren will be visiting *July 21* through *July 25.*

If you're writing the day before the month, write it out and use the ordinal.

the second of April, the Fourth of July

Remember the second comma after a year date.

June 7, 1944, was D-Day in France.

No commas are needed with just the month and the year.

June 1944   December '07

Be sure, if you're going to use an apostrophe to stand for the century, that your readers know from the context just which century you mean. December '07, for example, could mean December of 1907, 2007, or even 1607.

Put Commas Before Groups of 3 Numbers Except in Year Dates up to 9,999 and Numbers to the Right of a Decimal Point

Please bring a cashier's check for *$8,000* with you to the wedding.

Pi calculated to the 15th decimal place is *3.141592653589793.*

In the *1930s* there were no microwave ovens.

We think these cave paintings were done around *14,000* BC.

Spell Out Simple Fractions and Use Hyphens

Only *one-eighth* of the mayonnaise made it to the table: Joan ate the rest.

Birds spend half to *two-thirds* of their waking lives in a search for food.

Unless it begins a sentence, express a mixed fraction in figures.

Yes: I saw *4¾* movies yesterday: I couldn't watch the end of *The Matrix.*

No: I saw *four and three-fourths* movies yesterday: I couldn't watch the end of *The Matrix.*

Yes: *Two and one-half* hours later, John showed up with the lobsters.

No: *2½* hours later, John showed up with the lobsters.

Don't put *–th* or use the words *of a* after numerical fractions.

No: ¾ths cup

No: ¾ of a cup

Yes: ¾ cup

Put Footnote Numbers OUTSIDE All Punctuation Except a Dash

The article on plinth decoration by Judith Carter is useful here.[3]

The landing at Plymouth[2]—according to Bradford—was difficult.

Inclusive Numbers Have Special Rules

Inclusive numbers bracket a range of numbers, such as year dates, page numbers, and so forth.

❋ Carry over all the numerals that change, but include a minimum of two numerals.

1881–2008   1776–78   pages 14–16   pages 224–25   pages 225–304

NOTE: Use an en dash (–), not a hyphen.

❋ Do not use a mixture of words and en dashes with a range of numbers:

No: The meeting lasted *from 8:00–4:00.*

Yes: The meeting lasted *8:00–4:00.*

Yes: The meeting lasted *from 8:00 to 4:00.*

No: *Between 12–15* people came to the opening.

Yes: *Between 12 and 15* people came to the opening.

Worst of all: *Between 12 to 15 people* came to the opening.

✳ IN BRIEF

> Write the numbers one through nine as words; use numerals for 10 and greater.

> Exceptions to the numbers rule abound.

> If you have a mixture of numbers greater than and less than 10 referring to similar things, express them as either all numerals or all words.

> When two numbers are side by side, alternate between numerals and words.

> Write out rounded-off or approximate numbers.

> Rounded numbers greater than a million are written as a numeral plus a word.

> Write out a number at the beginning of a sentence.

> Write out people's ages except in scientific or technical copy.

> Numbers 21 through 99 are hyphenated when written out; larger numbers are not hyphenated.

> Don't use ordinal numbers when writing dates if the month comes before the day.

> Put commas before groups of three numbers except in year dates up to 9,999 and numbers to the right of a decimal point.

> Spell out simple fractions and use hyphens.

> Put footnote numbers OUTSIDE all punctuation except a dash.

> Inclusive numbers have special rules.

MAKE SURE YOU'VE GOT IT!

Choose the correct alternative in the following sentences.

1. Charlotte's plane lands at (4:17 p.m., four seventeen p.m.), and we're due at the dinner at (8:15, eight fifteen).

2. (1866, Eighteen sixty-six) was perhaps the most terrible year of all for the South.

3. The bathroom is (9, nine) by (12, twelve) feet.

4. *Science* magazine asserts that the Grand Canyon is (17,000,000, 17 million) years old, rather than (5,000,000 or 6,000,000, 5 or 6 million, five or six million) as was previously thought.

5. I went to (15, fifteen) different schools (between 1983-2000, between 1983 to 2000, between 1983 and 2000).

6. He promised to return on the (1st, first) of April.

7. Please order (4 36-inch, four 36-inch) brackets and (12 6-inch, twelve 6-inch) S hooks.

8. On Friday (5 mg, five mg) of Imipramine, a sub-therapeutic dose, was ordered.

9. (255, Two-hundred fifty-five, Two hundred fifty-five) men charged an army of about (2,000, two thousand).

10. The recipe calls for (¼ of a pound, ¼ pound, one-quarter of a pound) of butter.

11. Mary brought with her (seven dolls, 12 books, and three puzzles; 7 dolls, 12 books, and 3 puzzles; seven dolls, twelve books, and three puzzles).

12. The temperature was (32 degrees, thirty-two degrees) when I went swimming with George.

13. (September 25, September 25th) is Take Your Spathyphyllum to Work Day.

14. ($7.50, Seven dollars and fifty cents) was all the money we had between us.

15. Margaret Thatcher—Attila the Hen to some, not entirely without admiration—sent the British Navy to the Falklands in (April 1982, April, 1982).

Answer Key

1. Charlotte's plane lands at **4:17 p.m.,** and we're due at the dinner at **8:15.**

2. **Eighteen sixty-six** was perhaps the most terrible year of all for the South.

3. The bathroom is *9* by *12* feet.

4. *Science* magazine asserts that the Grand Canyon is *17 million* years old, rather than *5 or 6 million* as was previously thought.

5. I went to *15* different schools *between 1983 and 2000.*

6. He promised to return on the *first* of April.

7. Please order *four 36-inch* brackets and *twelve 6-inch* S hooks.

8. On Friday *5 mg* of Imipramine, a sub-therapeutic dose, was ordered.

9. *Two hundred fifty-five* men charged an army of about *two thousand.*

10. The recipe calls for *one-quarter of a pound* of butter. NOTE: IF THIS WERE AN INGREDIENT LISTED IN A RECIPE, IT WOULD BE WRITTEN AS *1/4 POUND.*

11. Mary brought with her *7 dolls, 12 books, and 3 puzzles.* OR Mary brought with her *seven dolls, twelve books, and three puzzles.*

12. The temperature was *32 degrees* when I went swimming with George.

13. *September 25* is Take Your Spathyphyllum to Work Day.

14. *Seven dollars and fifty cents* was all the money we had between us.

15. Margaret Thatcher—Attila the Hen to some, not entirely without admiration—sent the British Navy to the Falklands in *April 1982.*

Appendix:
For Further Reading

Here are some comprehensive and authoritative books that delve deeply into subjects I've discussed briefly in this book.

Chicago Manual of Style, 15th Edition (University of Chicago Press, 2003).

Surely the granddaddy of them all, this highly respected manual takes a writer through all the necessary steps to publication of a thesis or a novel. It probably tells you more than you need to know as a non-scholarly writer, but the information is so comprehensive and so dependable that I would never be without it.

A Manual for Writers of Research Papers, Theses, and Dissertations, 7th Edition, by Kate Turabian et al. (University of Chicago Press, 2007).

Based on the *Chicago Manual of Style*, this useful paperback contains information on capitalization, punctuation, and style issues. Like *Chicago*, it's written for scholars; the new material in this edition focuses on citation issues: footnotes, bibliography, and front matter, including online research and documentation.

Words into Type, 3rd Edition, edited by Marjorie Skillen and Robert Gay (Prentice Hall, 1974).

A must for copy editors, proofreaders, and professional writers. Don't let the long-ago publication date fool you. This one's never gone out of print. A fourth edition that came out in 1992 has vanished from the scene, elbowed out no doubt by the reader-friendly, clearly written third. *Words into Type* is targeted to people readying a manuscript for typeset or publication, but copy editors fid it helpful and authoritative, and it's organized and written in such a way that it's accessible to everyone.

Remember that dictionaries often contain usage information for troublesome words as well as definitions, pronunciation, and so forth. Trying to choose a dictionary among the hundreds can be overwhelming, particularly with all the wannabe Websters. (Don't be fooled: The dictionary needs to say **Merriam-**Webster, with the hyphen.) These are the two I use and recommend.

The American Heritage Dictionary of the English Language, 4th Edition (Houghton Mifflin Company, 2006; *www.bartleby.com/reference*).

In addition to everything a dictionary ought to have, this large and wonderful volume contains the opinions of its formidable Usage Panel on controversial words, notes on Word History, Regional Notes, and more than 4,000 pieces of illustrative art.

Merriam-Webster's Collegiate Dictionary, 11th Edition (Merriam-Webster, 2003; *www.merriam-webster.com*).

America's best-selling dictionary is also the *Chicago Manual of Style's* authority for issues of spelling and word division. New words added to this edition include *Botox* and *comb-over* (no comment). This is inarguably the definitive American arbiter of words. It is also the only place I've ever found that tells you how to address an envelope to an abbot.

If you like dictionaries, you might have some fun with *www.onelook.com/.* This dictionary search engine sorts through 109 dictionaries, in English and other languages, to help you find synonyms, antonyms, related words, whatever.

Index

About the Author

Becky Burckmyer has enjoyed a lifelong (well, not yet) fascination with the English language, ever since a Eureka moment involving the derivation of the word tricycle. Raised in Virginia in a family that cares passionately about language (poetry, correct grammar, words in all contexts), she graduated from Wellesley College with a BA in English and earned her MS in Library Science from Simmons College.

For more than 20 years Becky has consulted on various aspects of writing, as a writer, copy editor, one-on-one writing coach, and seminar leader. She designed and taught a number of courses for middle and upper-level management, including Business Writing for Senior Managers, Responding to Customer Complaints, and E-Mail Etiquette at Work. She has worked primarily with customers in the greater Boston area, such as Analog Devices, Eastern Bank, Fidelity Investments, Fleet Financial Services, John Hancock, and the National Association of Independent Schools. She has written innumerable articles for in-house newsletters for the banking and insurance industry as well as for some major newspapers and minor magazines. She has also served as copy editor for countless quarterly and annual reports, magazines, corporate newsletters, and full-length books. Becky's *Why Does My Boss Hate My Writing?* was published by Adams Media and published subsequently by Barnes & Noble.

Twenty-odd years of dealing with incorrect writing has only increased her sense of the importance of expressing oneself with scrupulous accuracy.

Becky lives with her husband, Larry, in Marblehead, Massachusetts. Besides finding fault with other people's copy, Becky's interests include reading (she's belonged to the same book club for 34 years), opera, Sudoku, sailing, beachcombing, and family.